HEALTHY HOMEMADE SOUPS

Recipes belong to

....

....

....

The Healthy Homemade Soups is one of the eight cookbooks published as part of a larger collection designed to help you write your own recipes in one place and have them at hand when you cook your favorite meals.

This **Special Collection** also includes:

- SALADS
- PASTRIES
- APPETIZERS
- DIET RECIPES
- OVEN RECIPES
- VEGAN RECIPES
- CAKES AND PIES

# Table of Contents

Recipe	Page

Table of Contents

Recipe	Page

Table of Contents

Recipe	Page

Table of Contents

Recipe	Page

Table of Contents

Recipe	Page

Recipe:____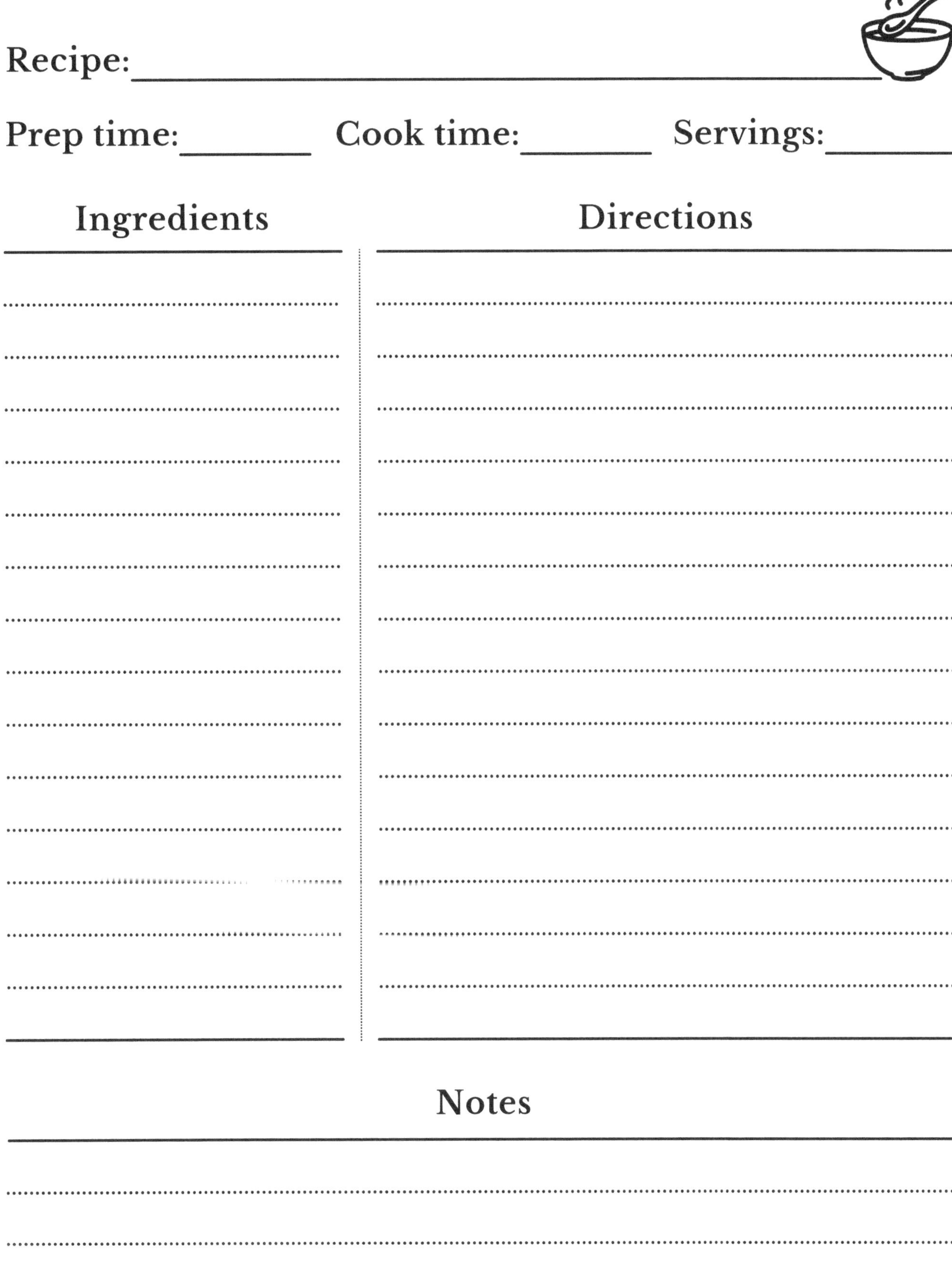

Prep time:________   Cook time:________   Servings:________

Ingredients

Directions

Notes

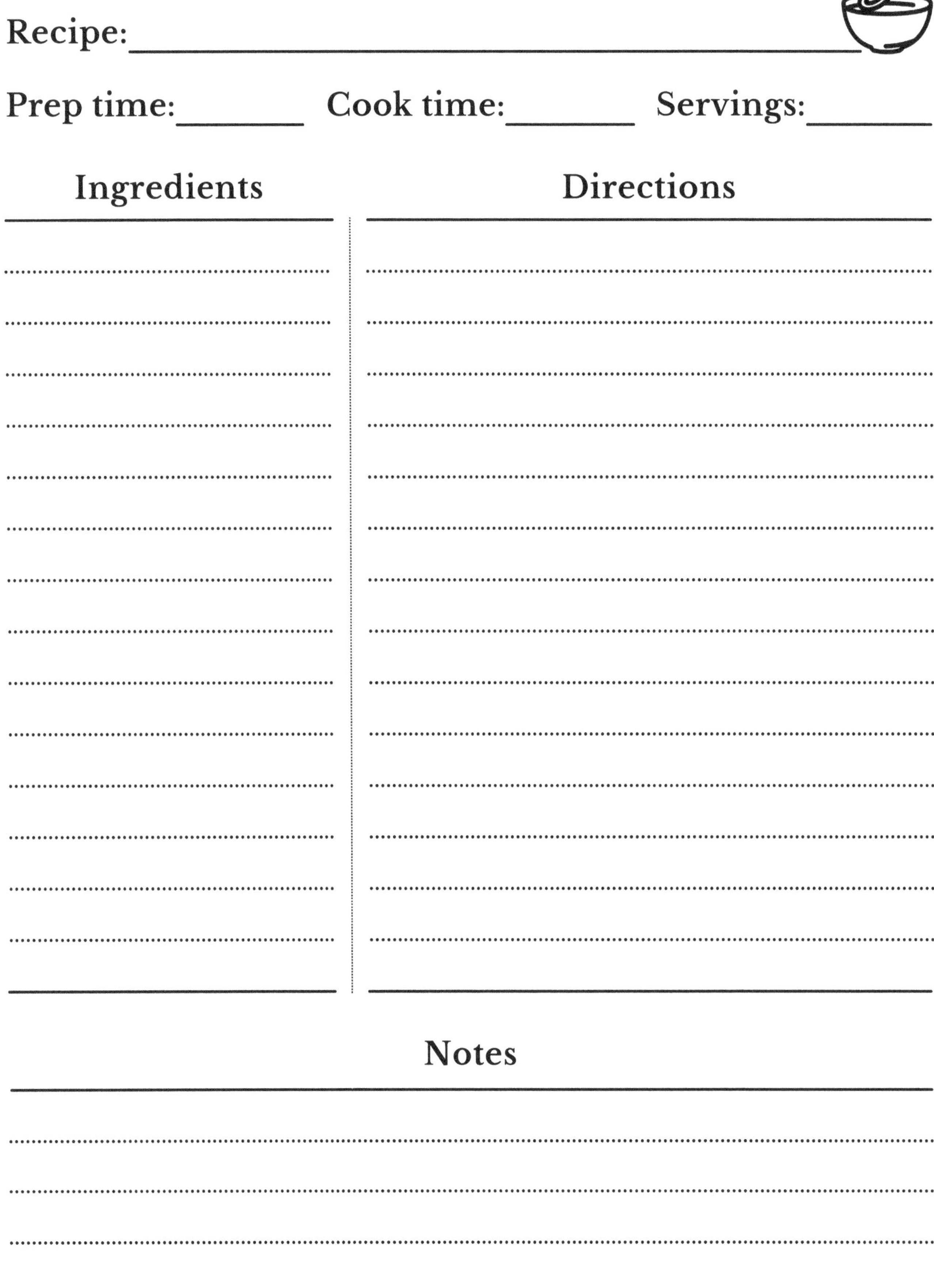

Recipe:____________________________________

Prep time:________ Cook time:________ Servings:________

Ingredients

Directions

Notes

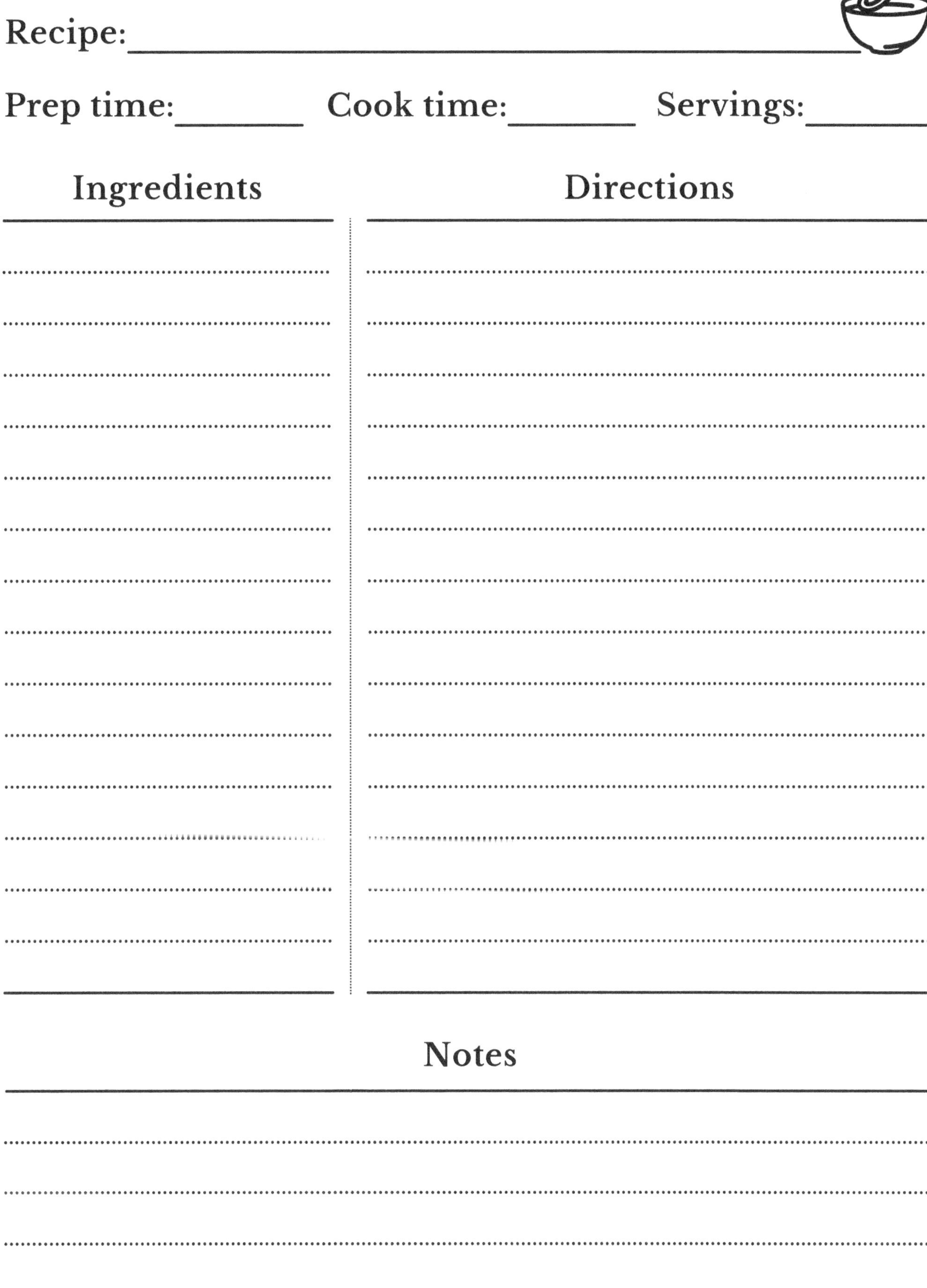

Recipe:____

Prep time:________ Cook time:________ Servings:________

| Ingredients | Directions |

Notes

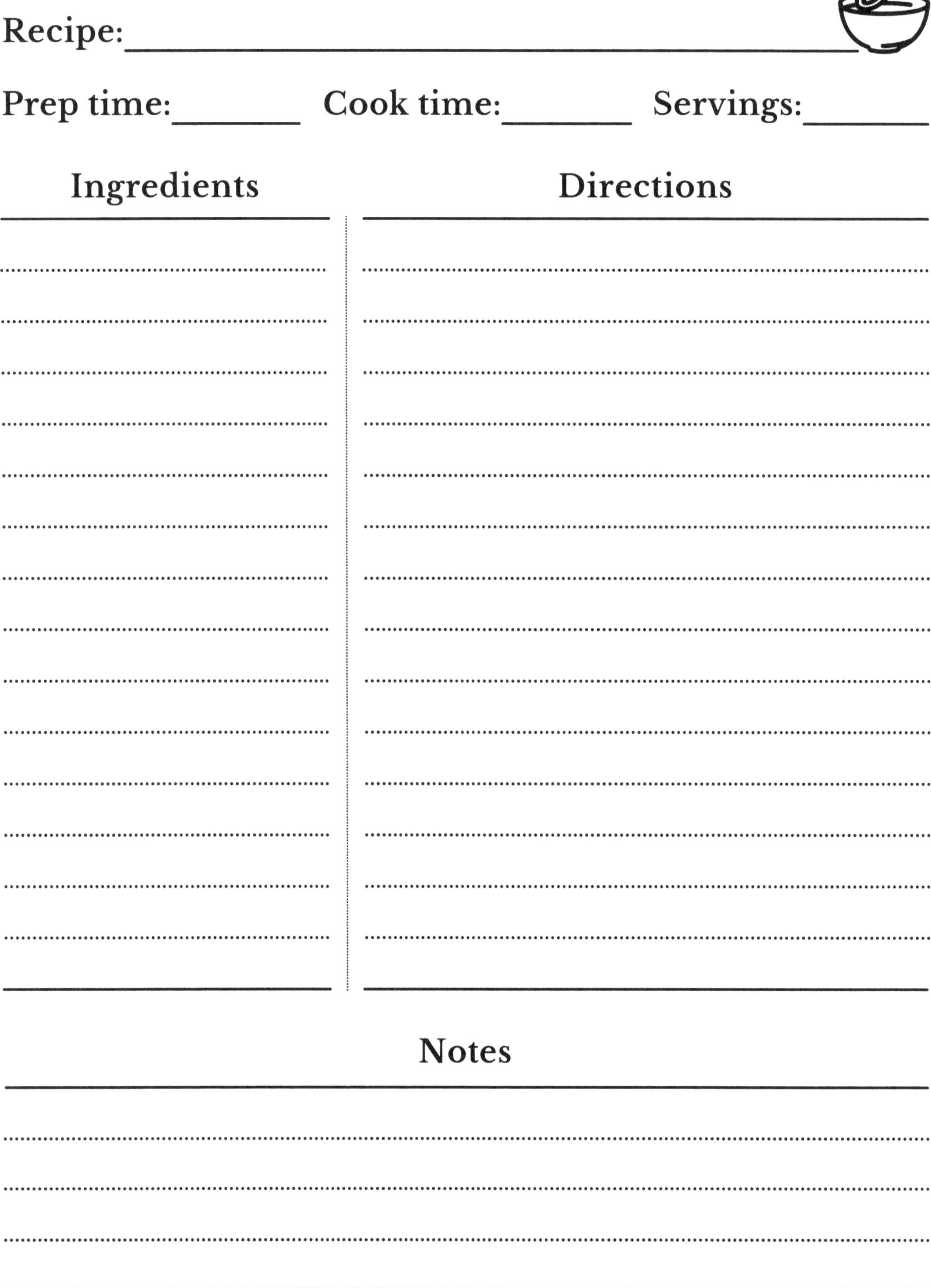

Recipe:____

Prep time:______ Cook time:______ Servings:______

Ingredients

Directions

Notes

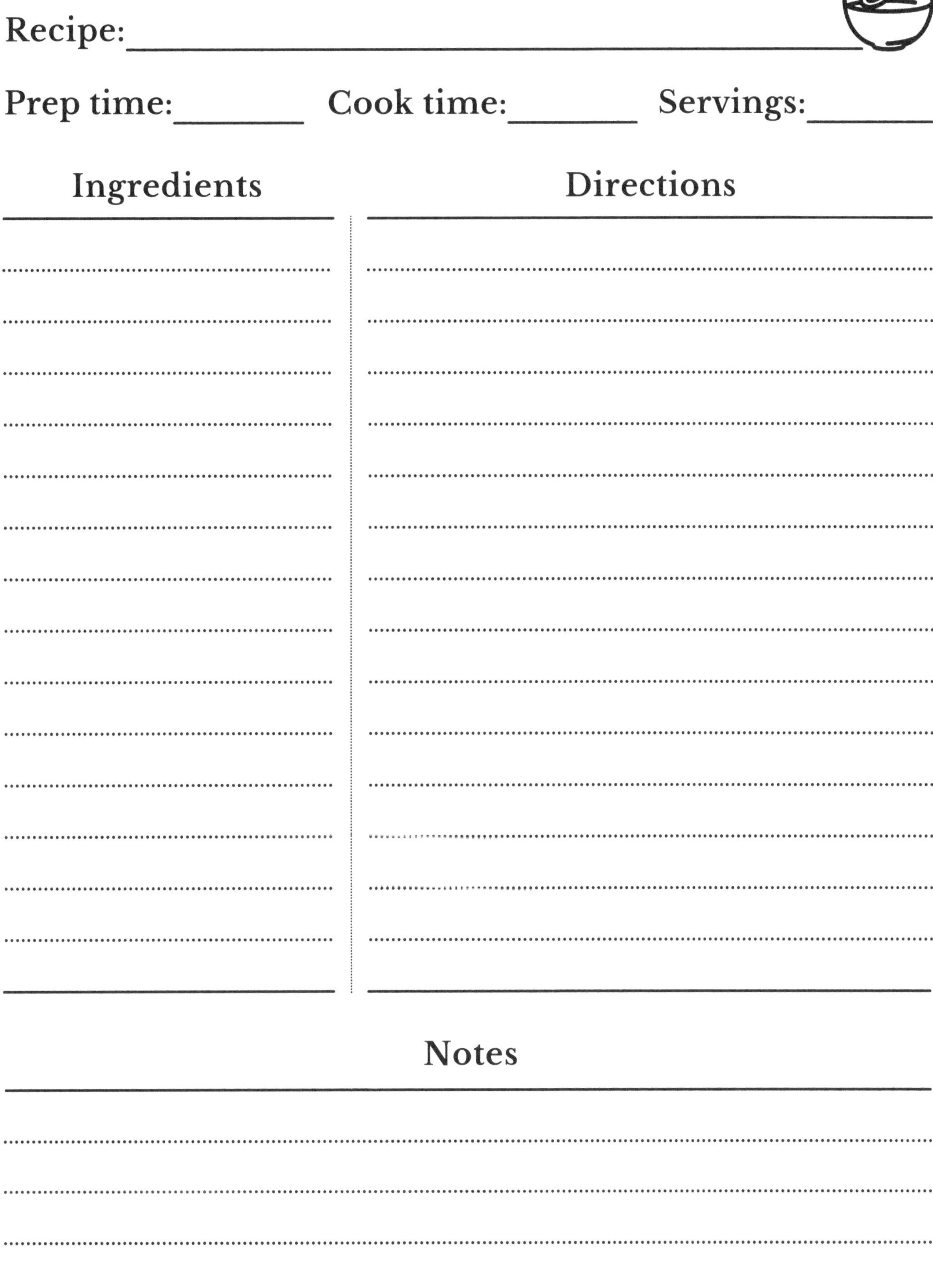

Recipe:___________________________________

Prep time:_______   **Cook time:**_______   **Servings:**_______

Ingredients	Directions

Notes

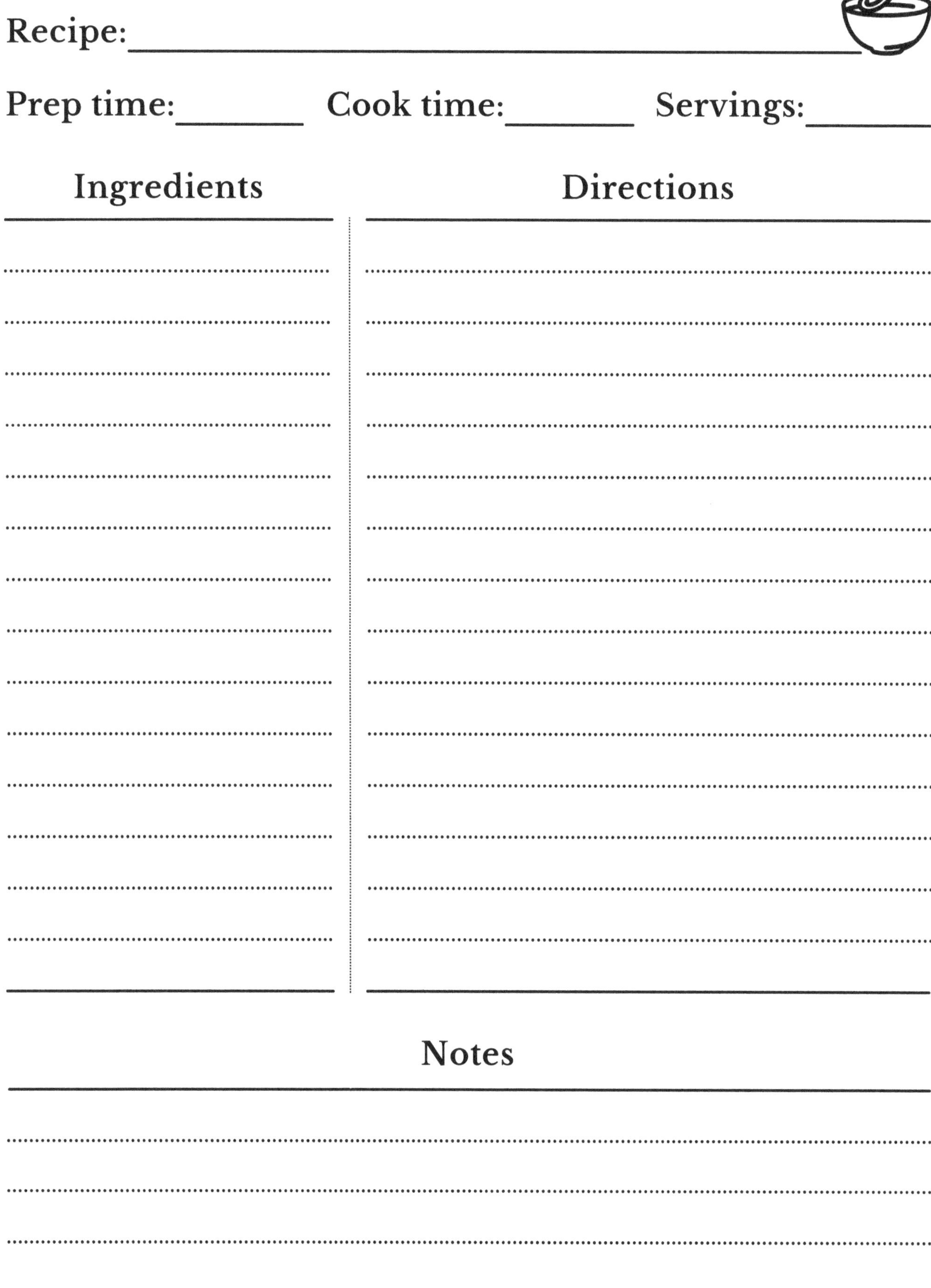

Recipe:_______________________________________

Prep time:_______   Cook time:_______   Servings:_______

Ingredients

Directions

Notes

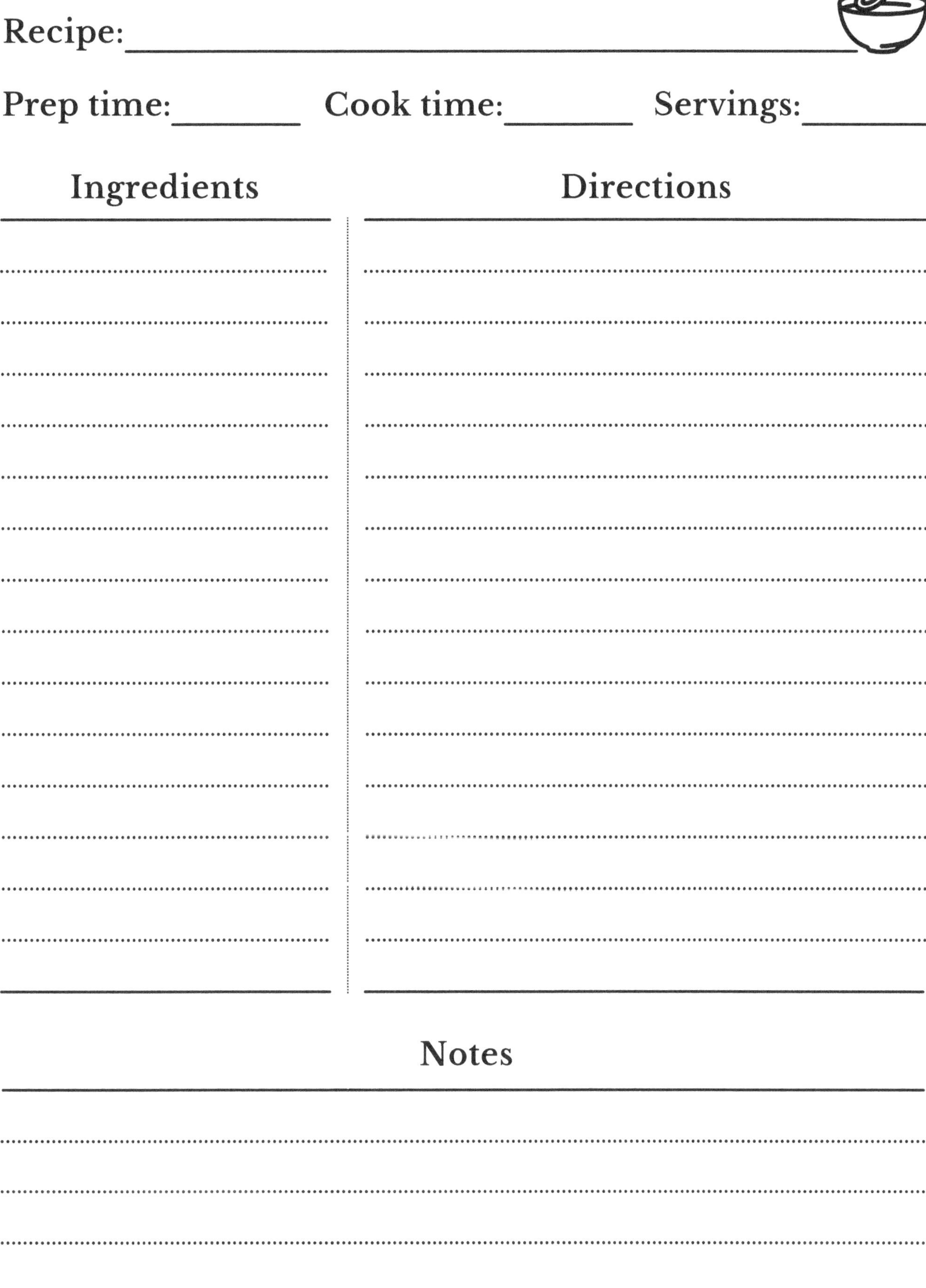

Recipe:____

Prep time:________   Cook time:________   Servings:________

Ingredients

Directions

Notes

Recipe:____

Prep time:_______   Cook time:_______   Servings:_______

Ingredients	Directions

Notes

Recipe:_______________________________________

Prep time:________ Cook time:________ Servings:________

Ingredients	Directions

Notes

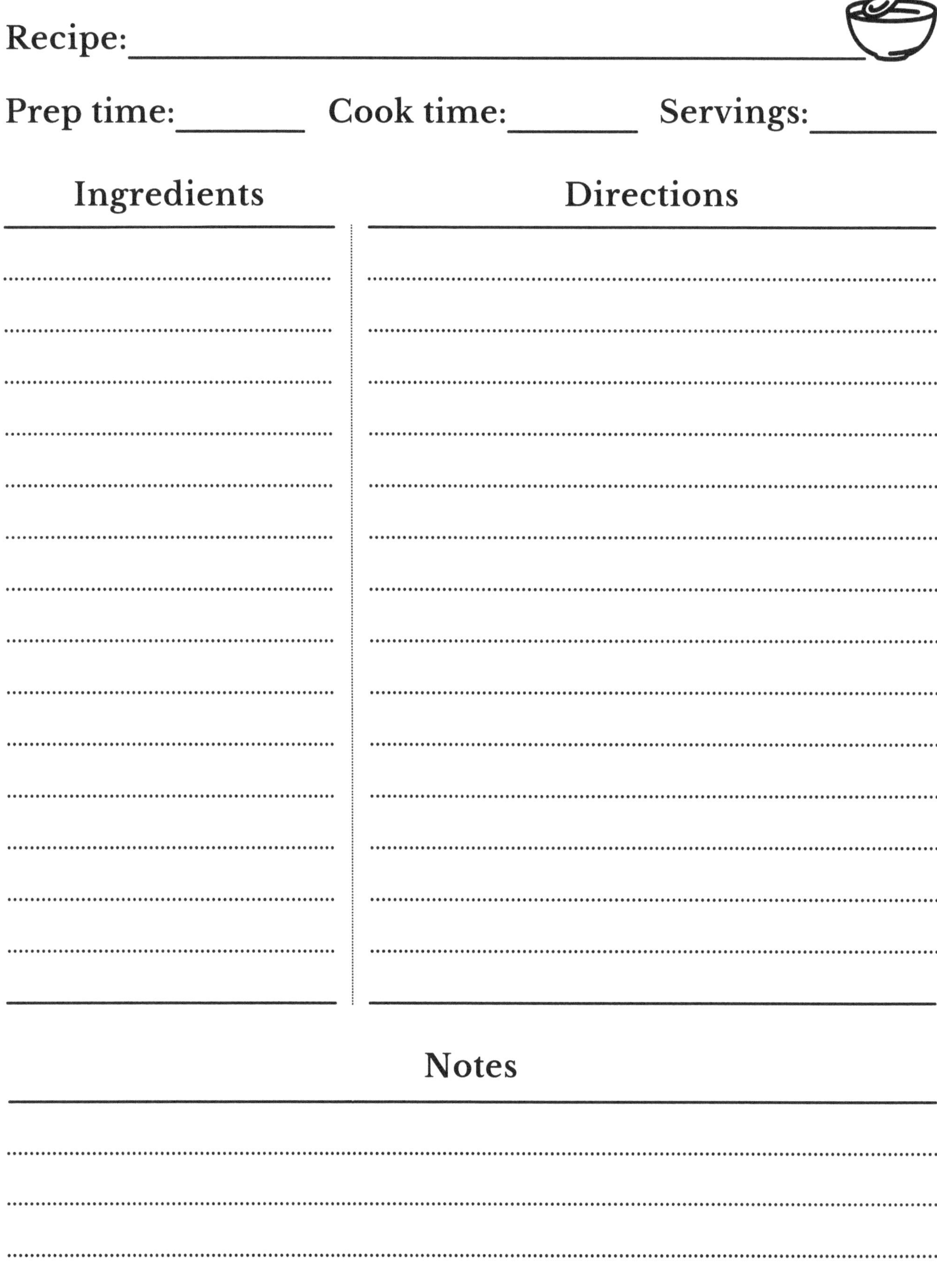

Recipe:____

Prep time:_______   Cook time:_______   Servings:_______

Ingredients

Directions

Notes

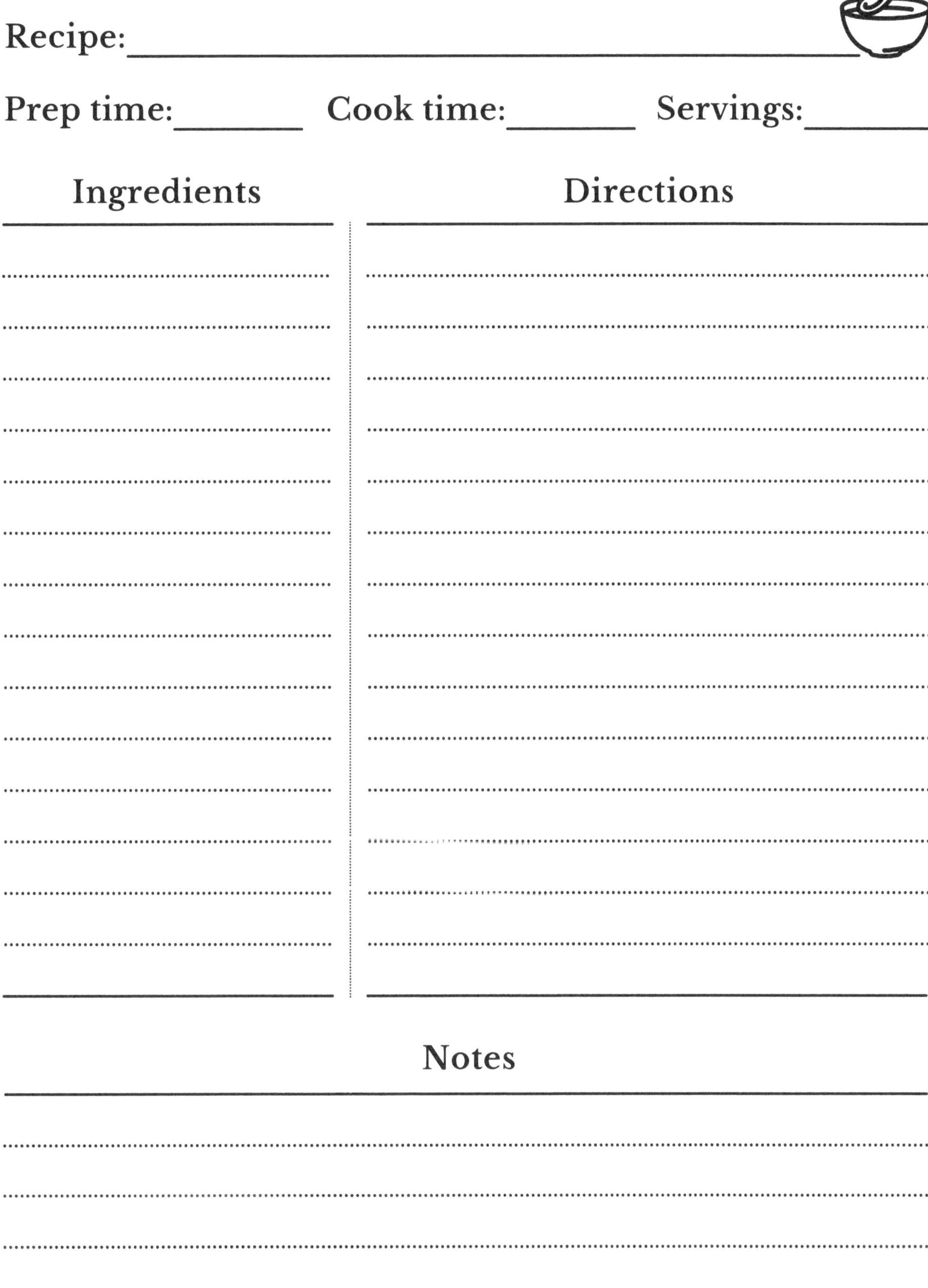

Recipe:

Prep time: Cook time: Servings:

Ingredients

Directions

Notes

Recipe:____ 

Prep time:________ Cook time:________ Servings:________

Ingredients | ## Directions

Notes

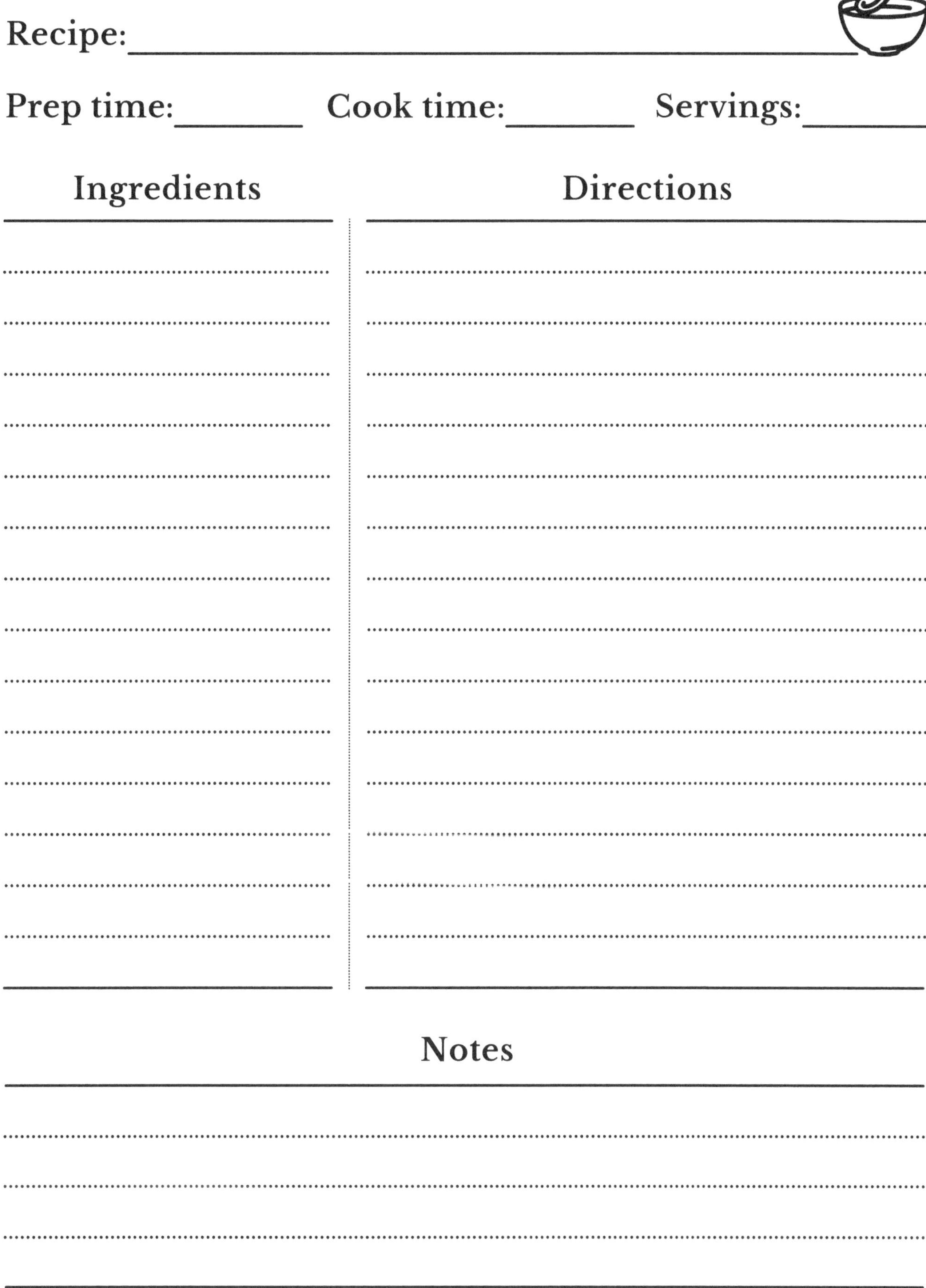

Recipe:_______________________________

Prep time:_______ Cook time:_______ Servings:_______

Ingredients

Directions

Notes

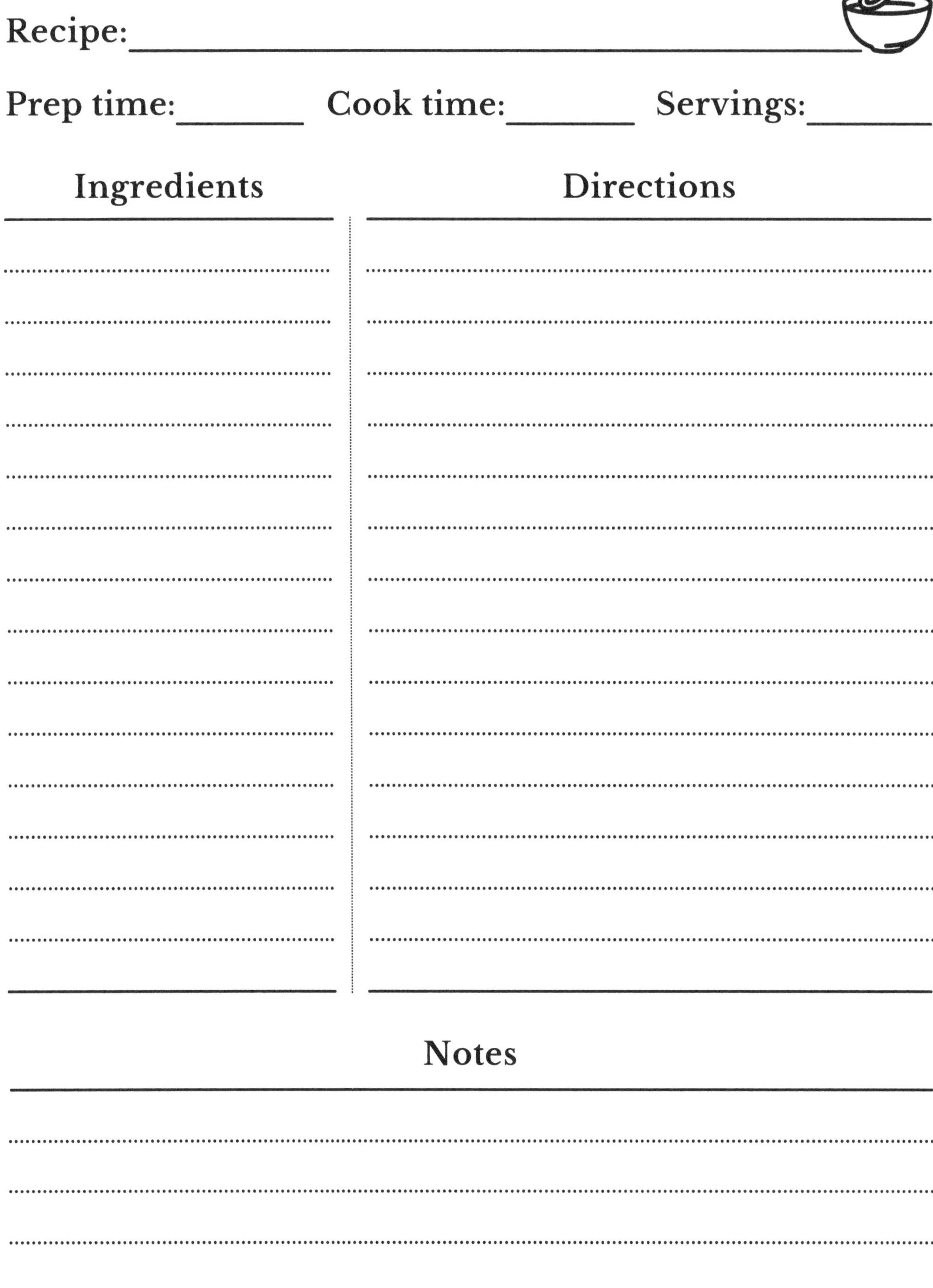

Recipe:____

Prep time:________   Cook time:________   Servings:________

Ingredients

Directions

Notes

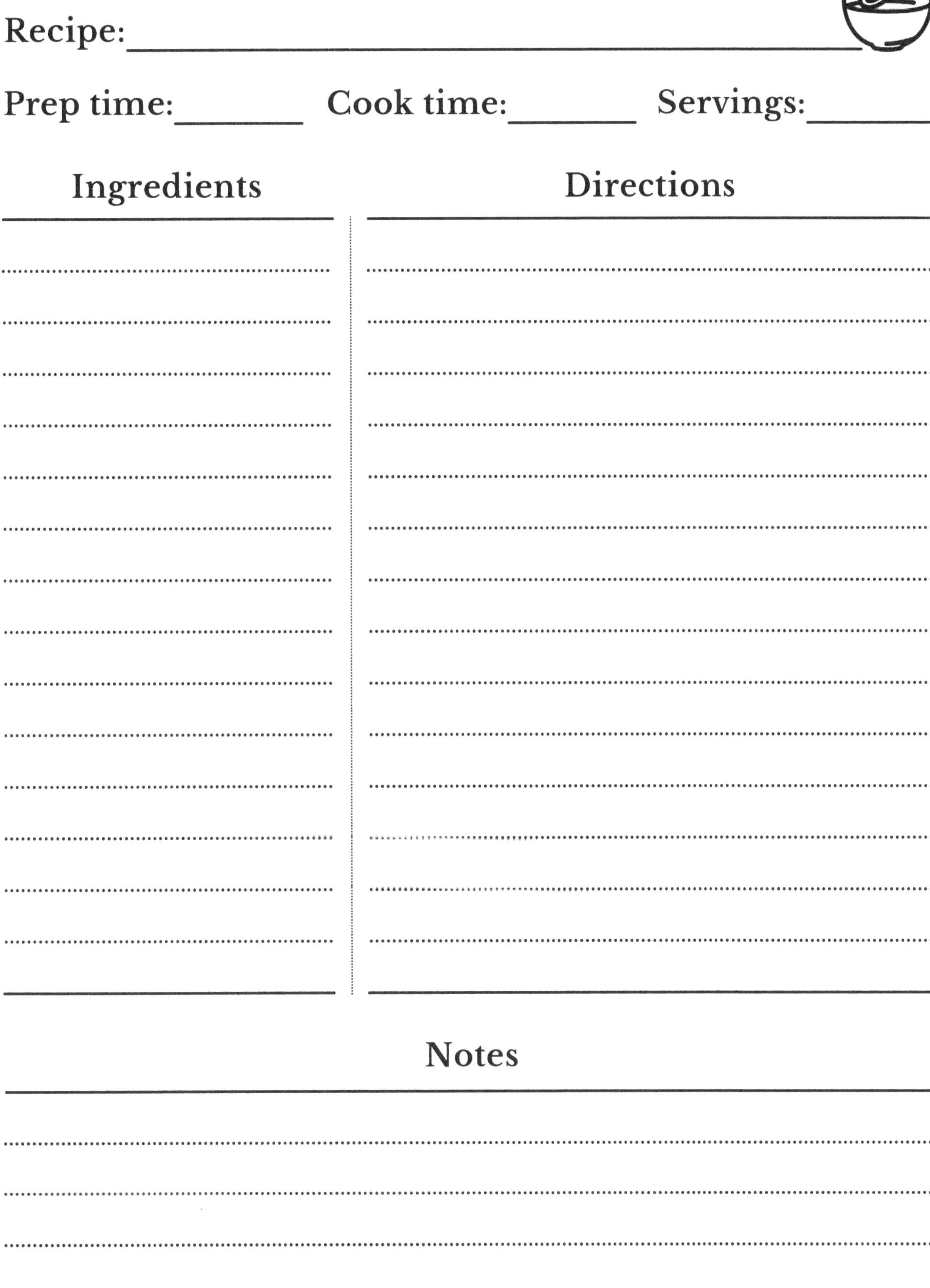

Recipe:____

Prep time:________   Cook time:________   Servings:________

Ingredients

Directions

Notes

Recipe:____ 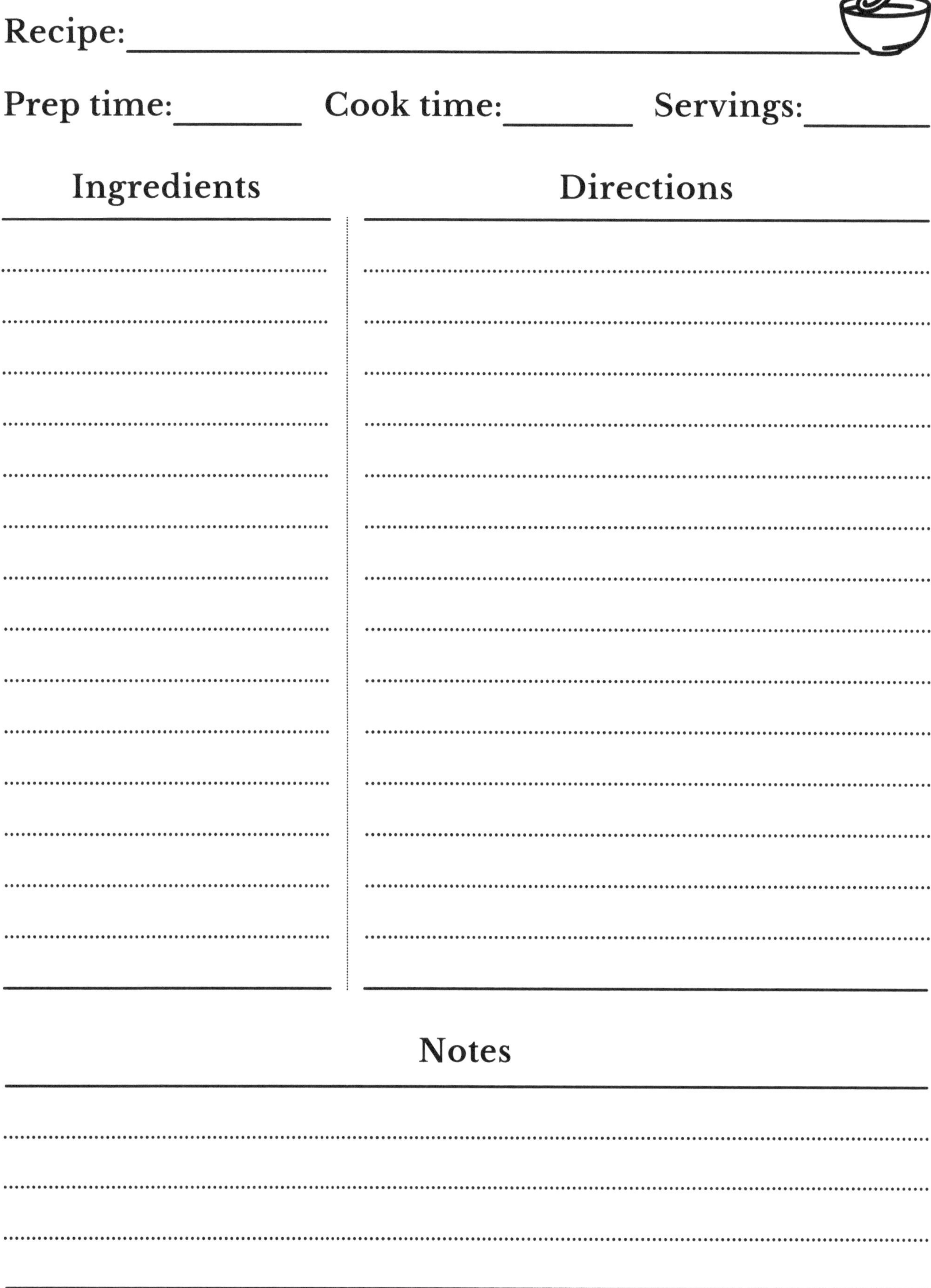

Prep time:________ Cook time:________ Servings:________

Ingredients

Directions

Notes

Recipe:____

Prep time:________   Cook time:________   Servings:________

Ingredients

Directions

Notes

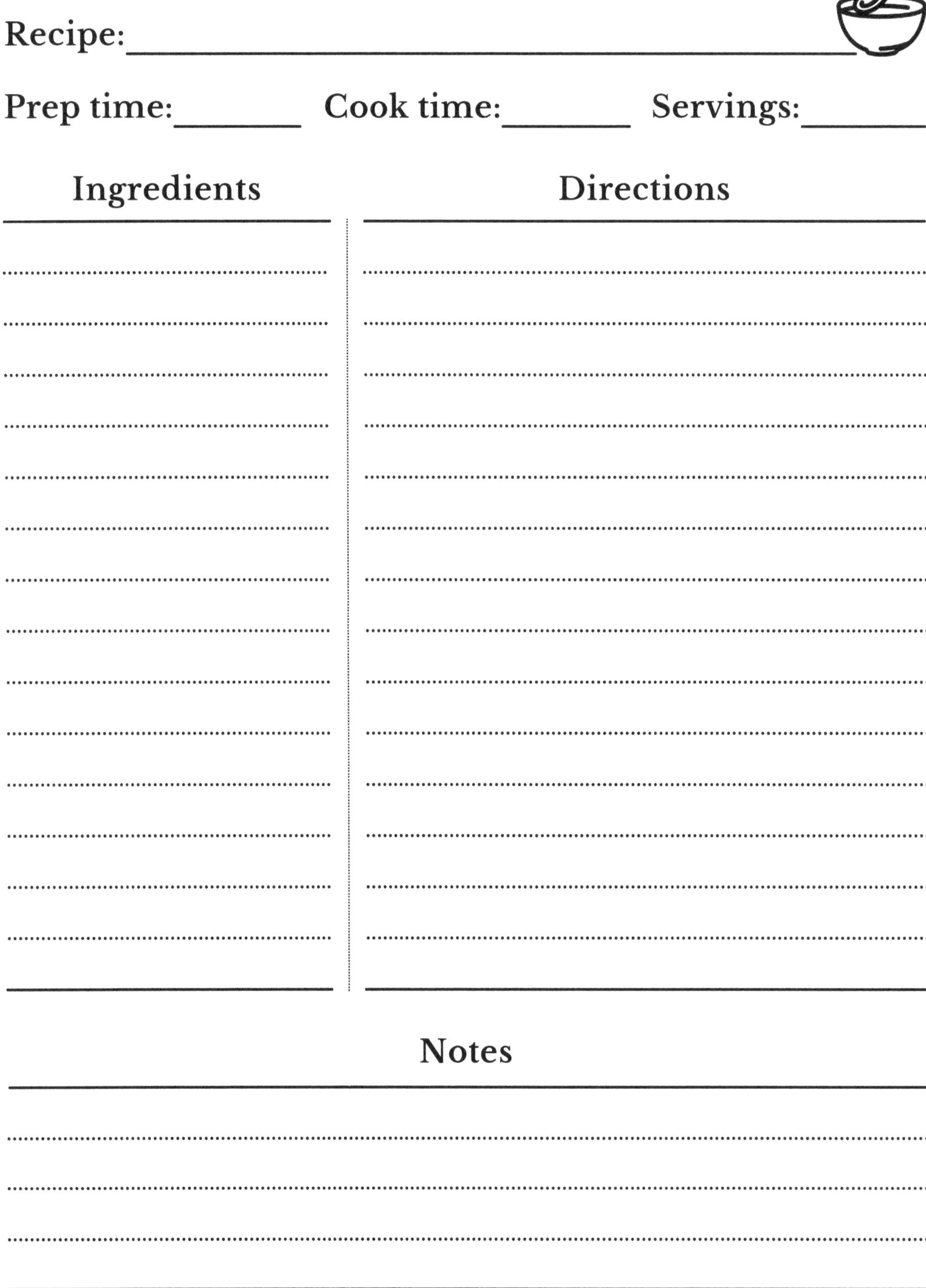

Recipe:__________

Prep time:______ Cook time:______ Servings:______

Ingredients

Directions

Notes

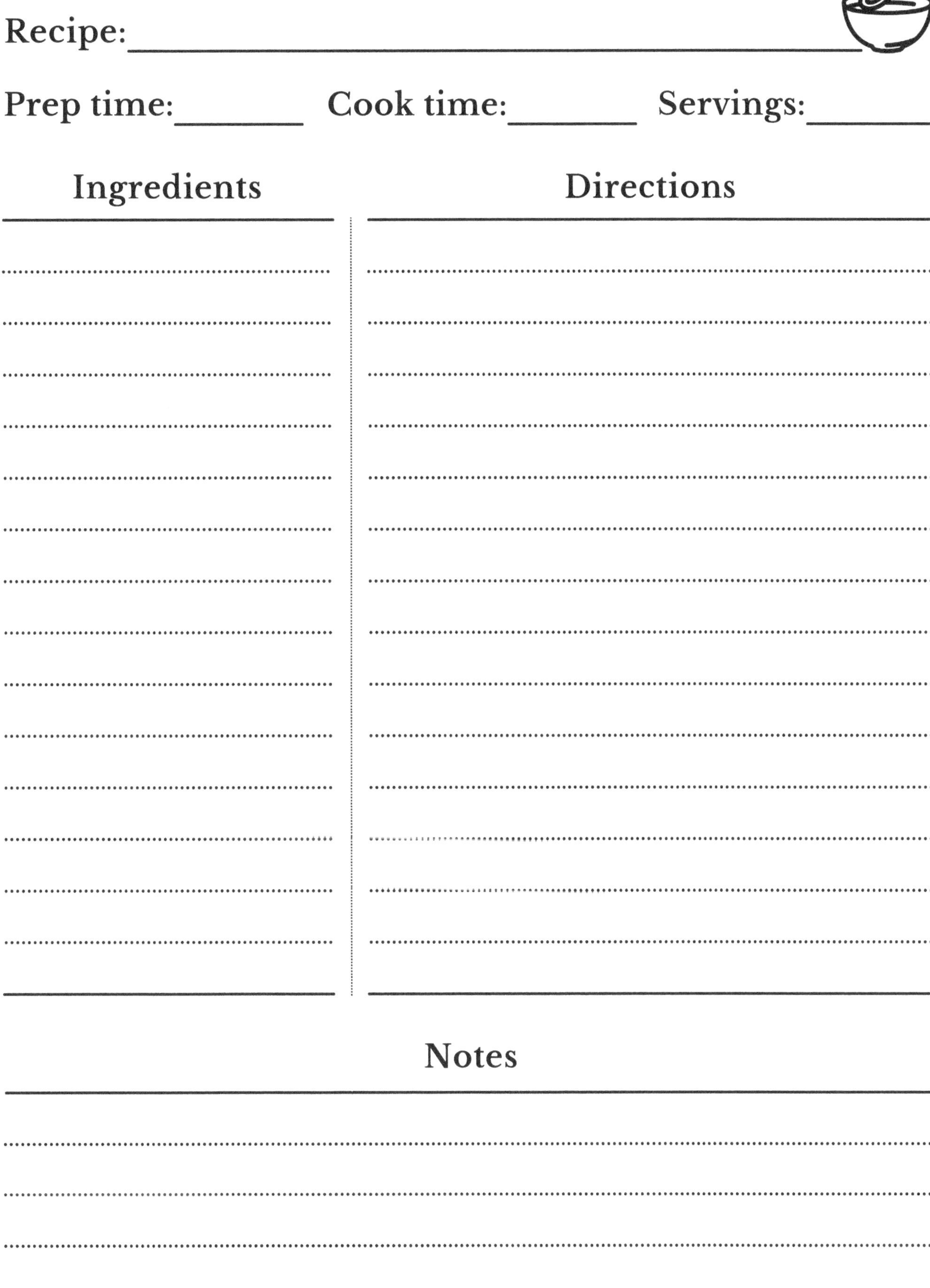

Recipe:________________________________

Prep time:________ Cook time:________ Servings:________

Ingredients

Directions

Notes

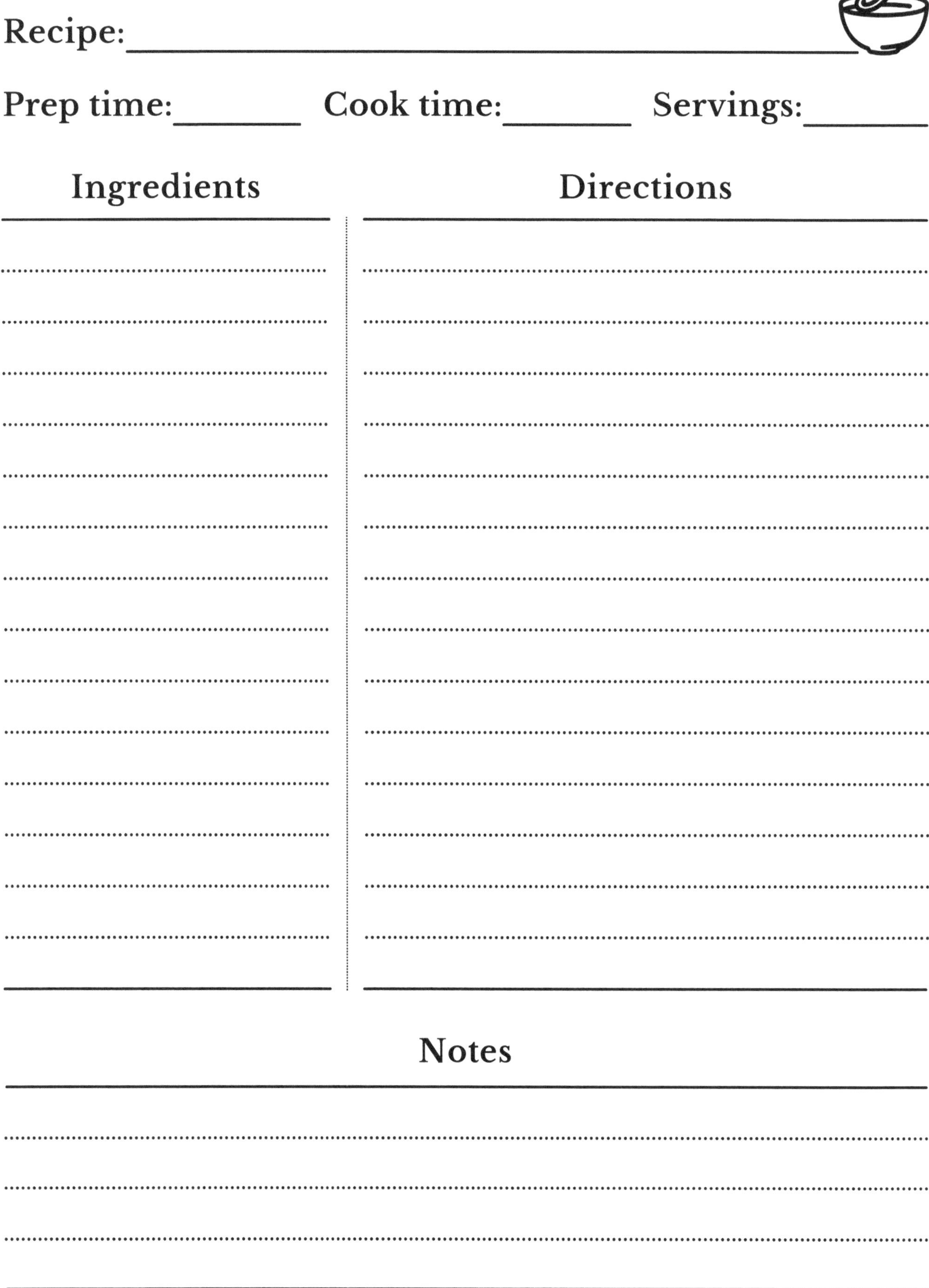

Recipe:____

Prep time:________ Cook time:________ Servings:________

Ingredients

Directions

Notes

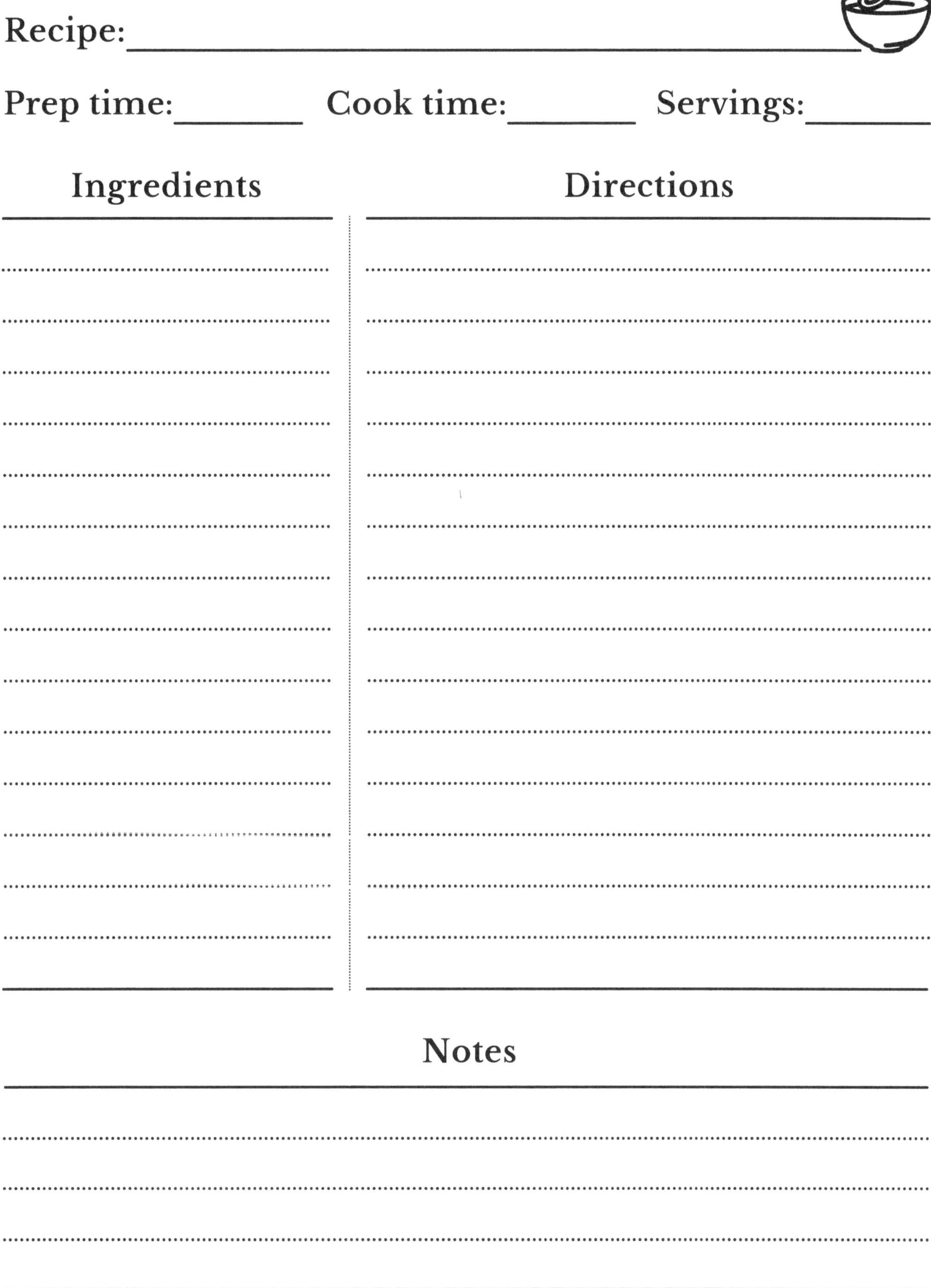

Recipe:____

Prep time:_______   Cook time:_______   Servings:_______

Ingredients

Directions

Notes

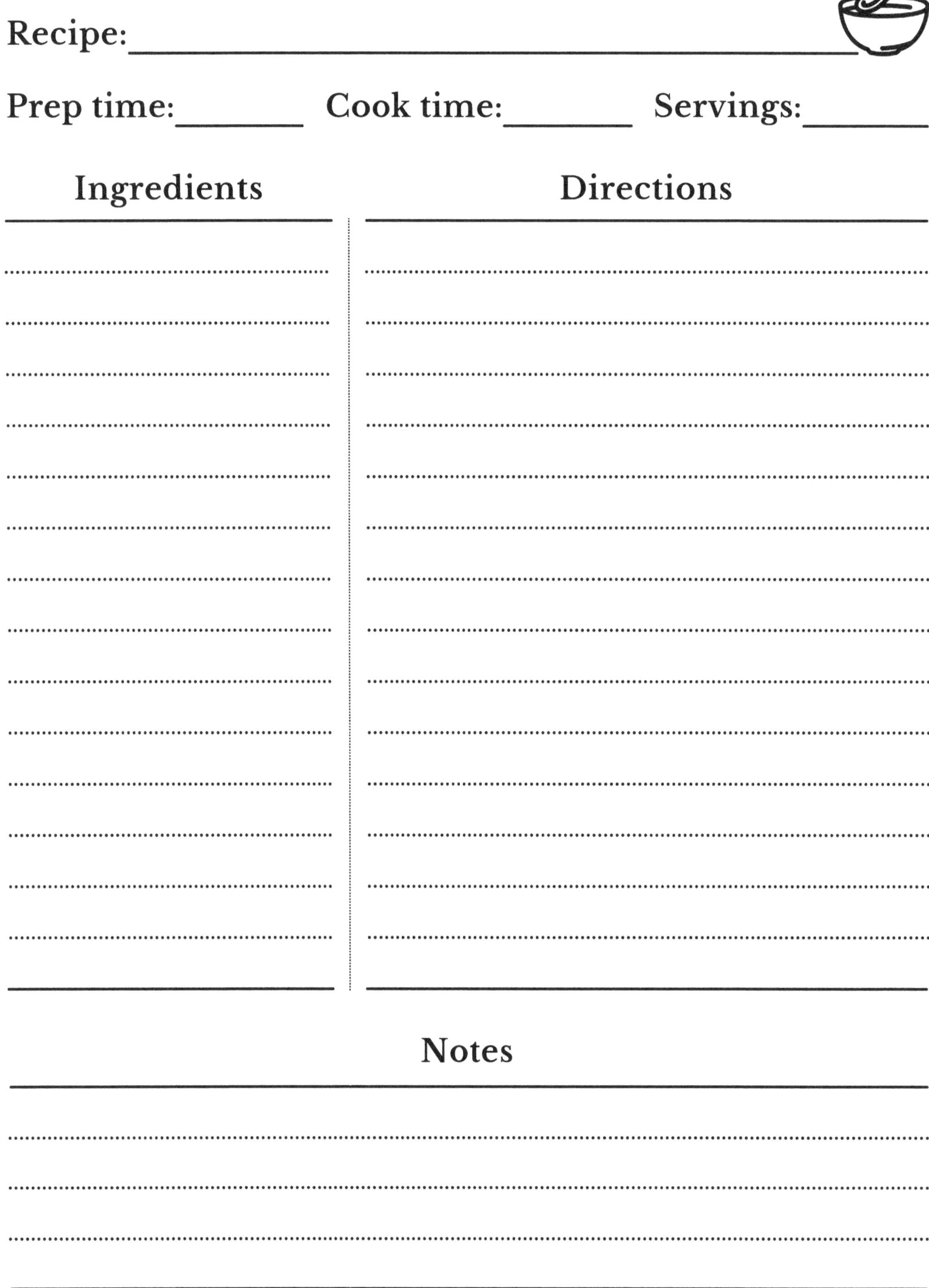

Recipe:____

Prep time:_______ Cook time:_______ Servings:_______

Ingredients

Directions

Notes

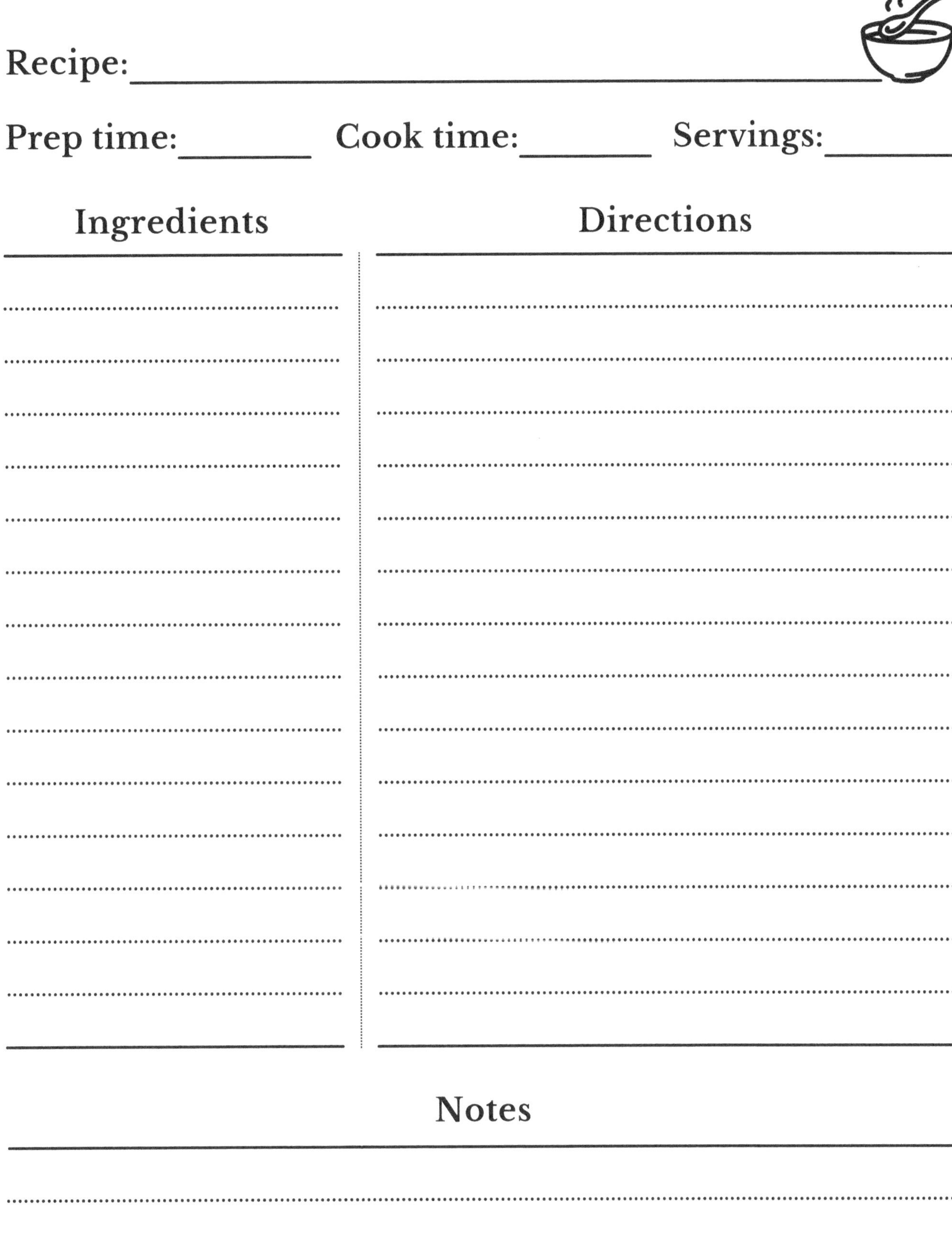

Recipe:____

Prep time:________   Cook time:________   Servings:________

Ingredients

Directions

Notes

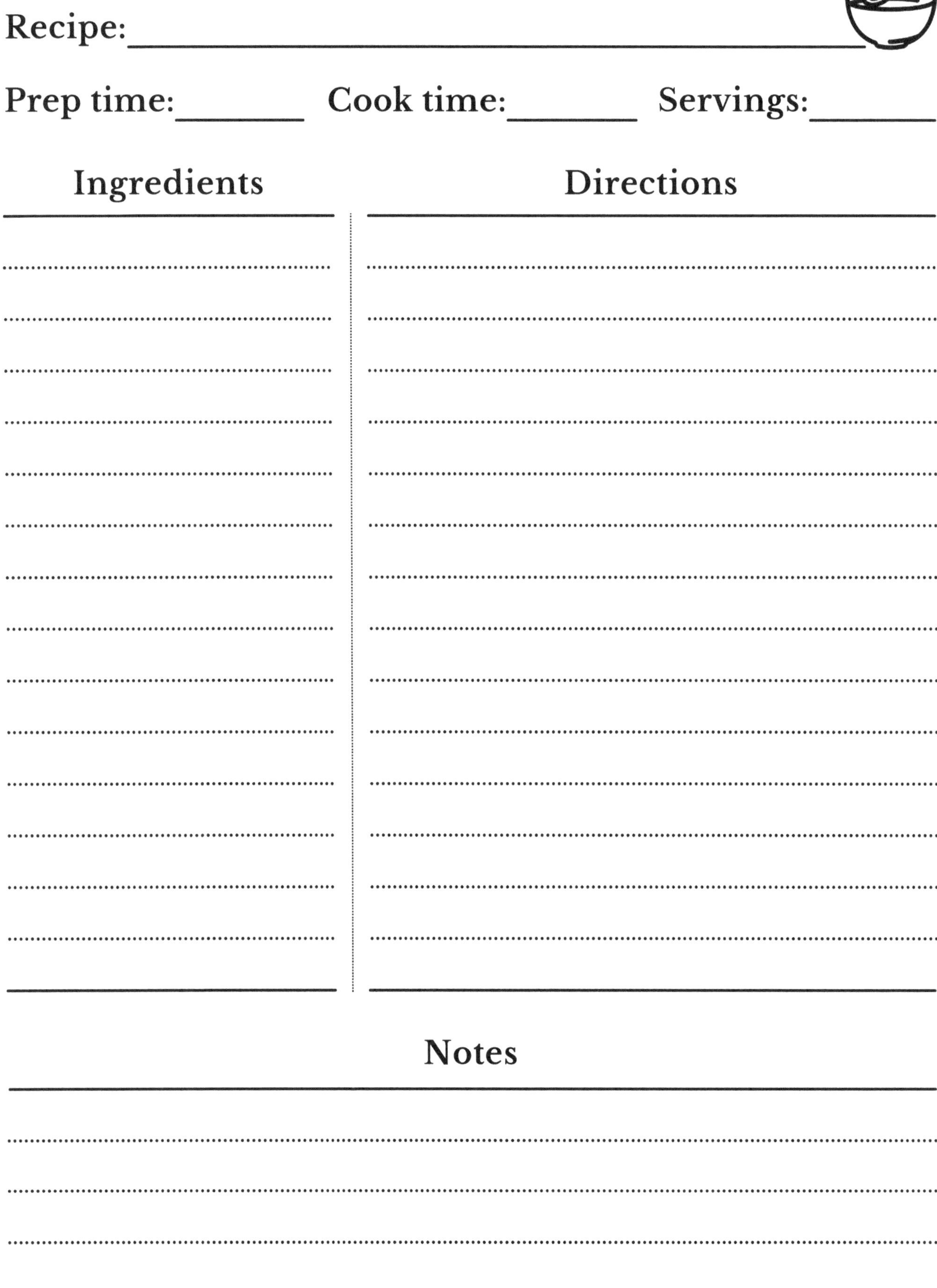

Recipe:______________________________

Prep time:______ Cook time:______ Servings:______

Ingredients

Directions

Notes

Recipe:____ 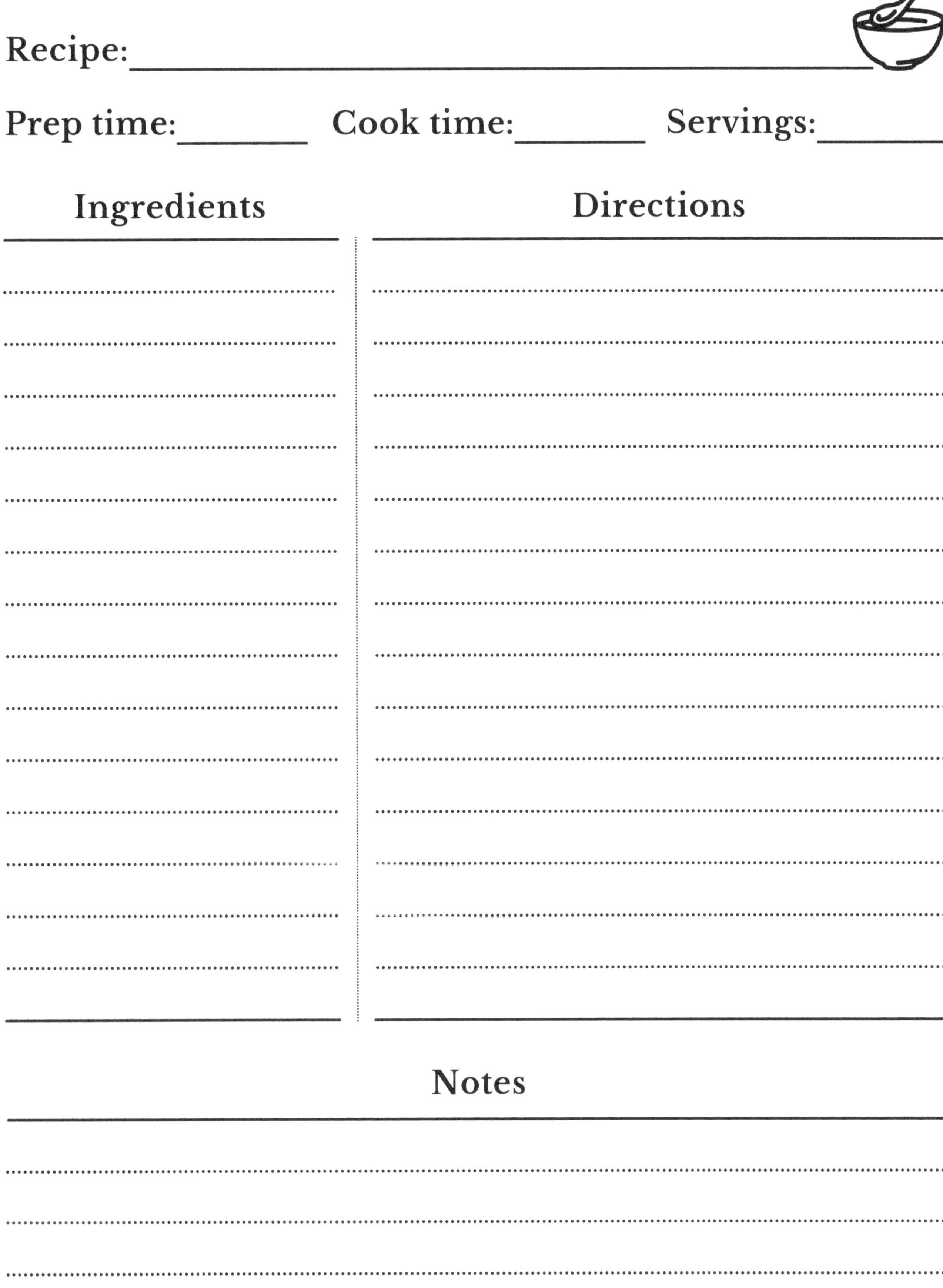

Prep time:________ Cook time:________ Servings:________

Ingredients | Directions

Notes

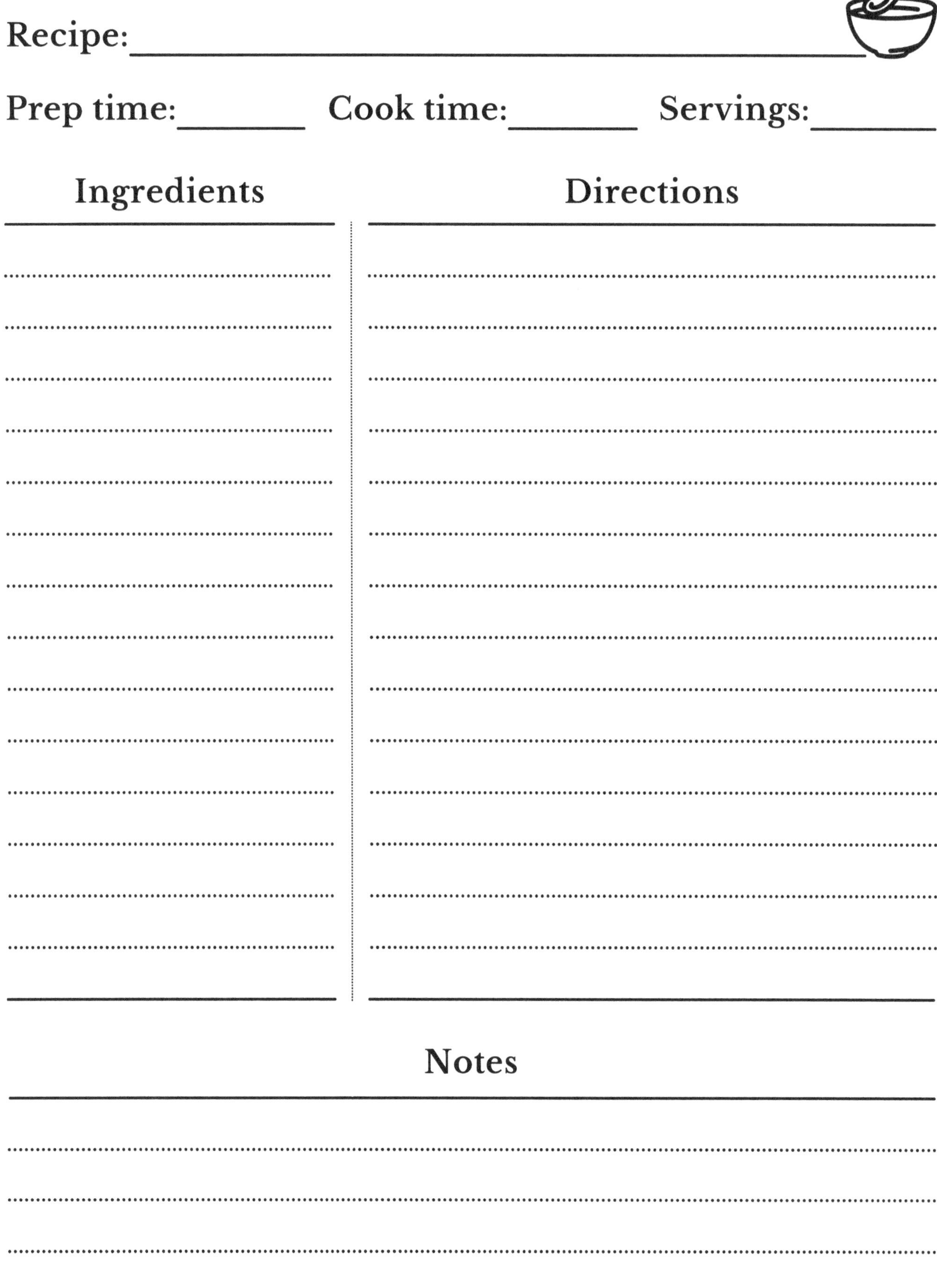

Recipe:_______________________________________

Prep time:________   Cook time:________   Servings:________

Ingredients

Directions

Notes

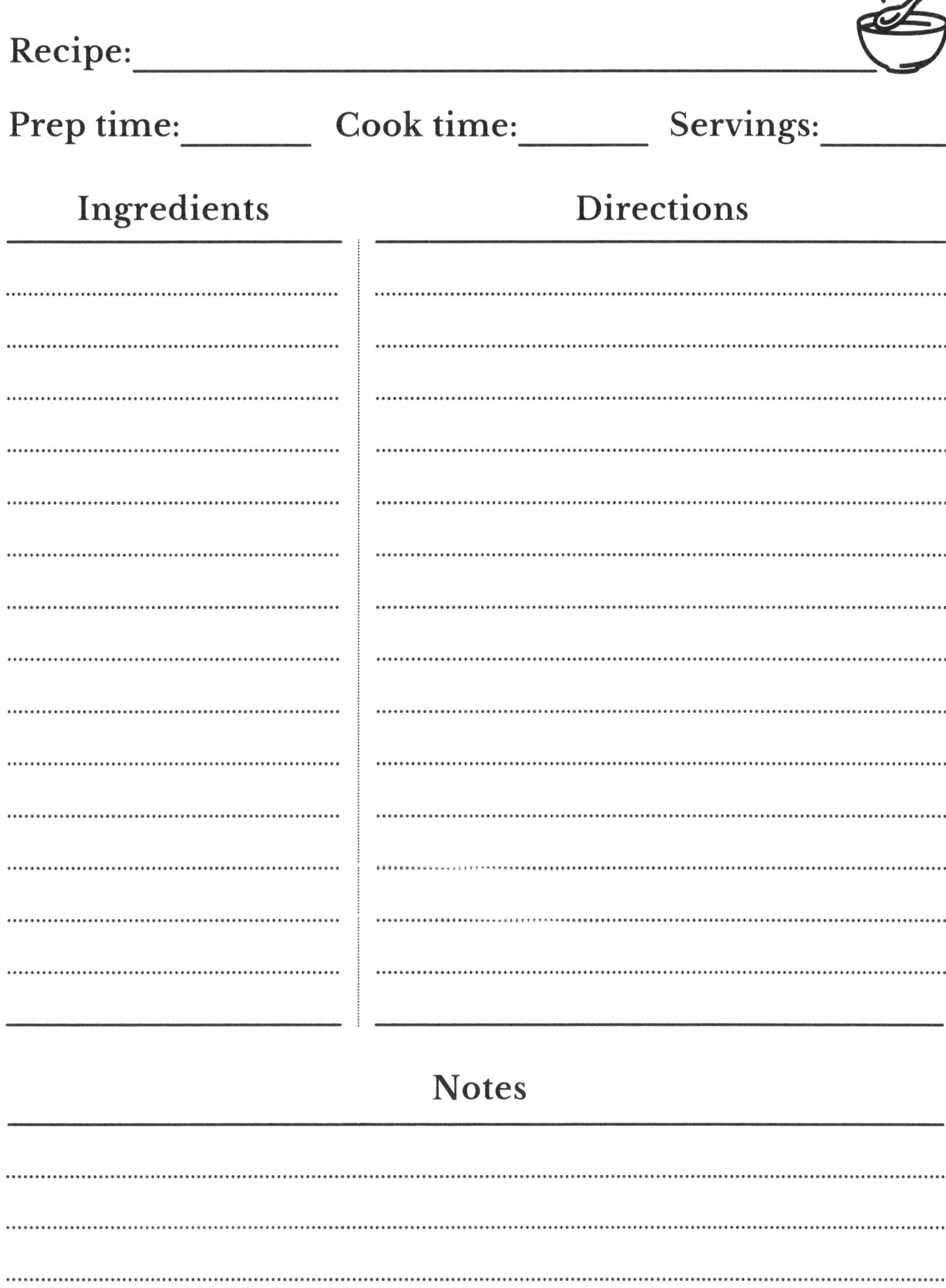

Recipe:_______________________________________

Prep time:________ Cook time:________ Servings:________

Ingredients	Directions

Notes

Recipe:____ 

Prep time:_______   Cook time:_______   Servings:_______

Ingredients

Directions

Notes

Recipe:____

Prep time:_______   Cook time:_______   Servings:_______

Ingredients

Directions

Notes

Recipe:____

Prep time:_________ Cook time:_________ Servings:_________

Ingredients

Directions

Notes

Recipe:____

Prep time:_______   Cook time:_______   Servings:_______

Ingredients

Directions

Notes

Recipe:_______________________________ 

Prep time:_______ Cook time:_______ Servings:_______

Ingredients

Directions

Notes

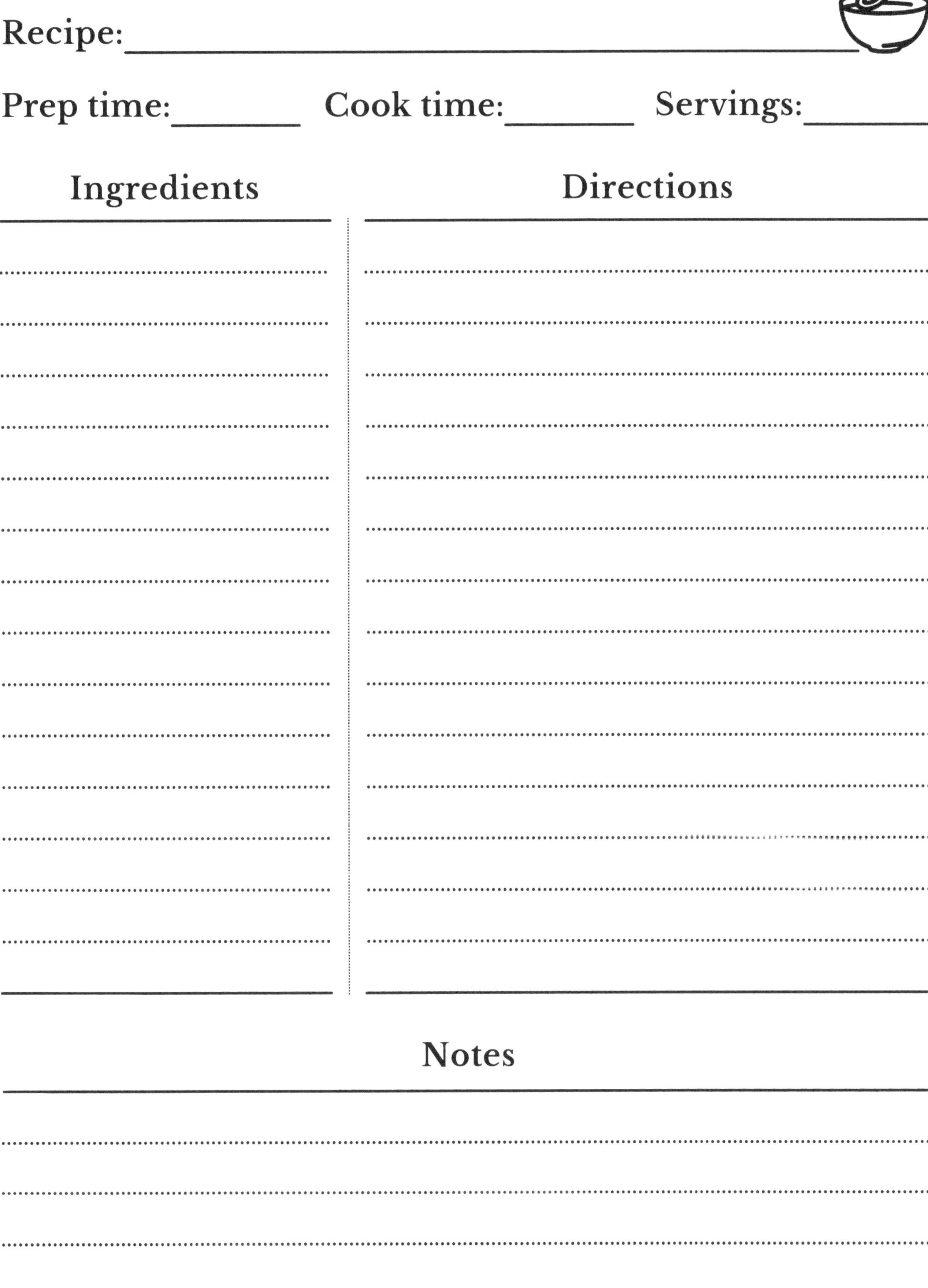

Recipe:____

Prep time:________ Cook time:________ Servings:________

Ingredients

Directions

Notes

Recipe: _______________________

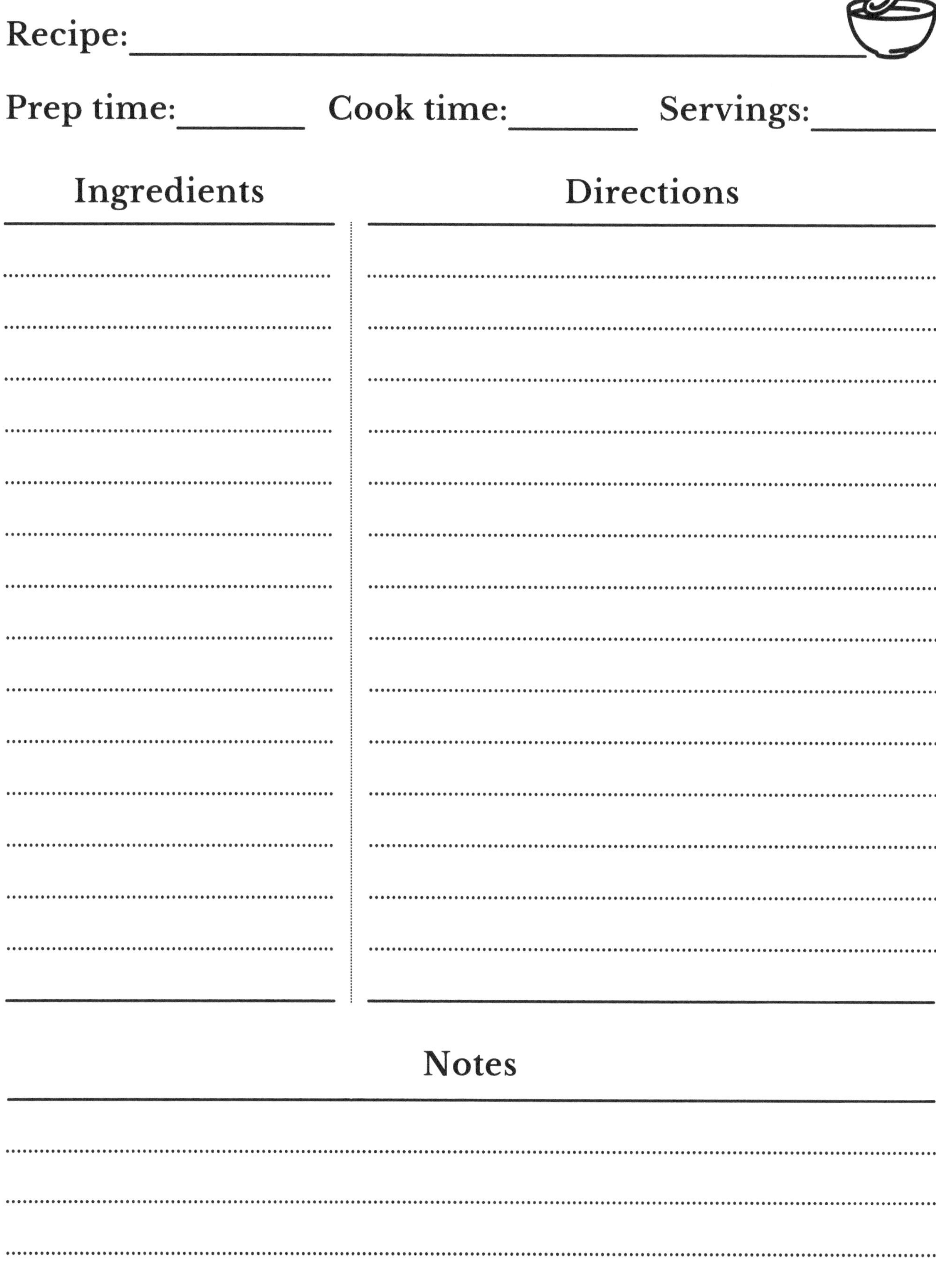

Prep time: ______   Cook time: ______   Servings: ______

Ingredients

Directions

Notes

Recipe:____ 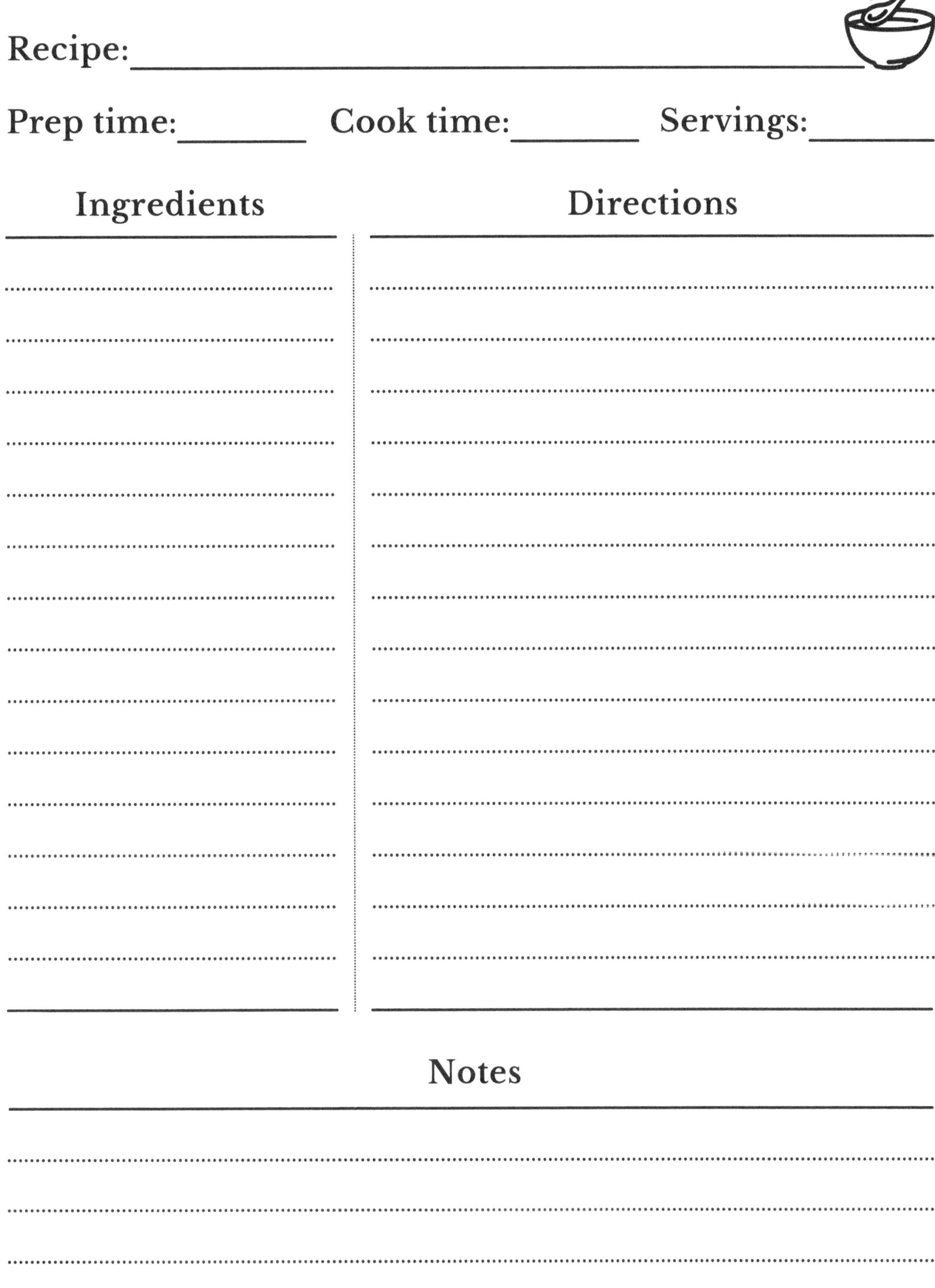

Prep time:________ Cook time:________ Servings:________

Ingredients | ## Directions

Notes

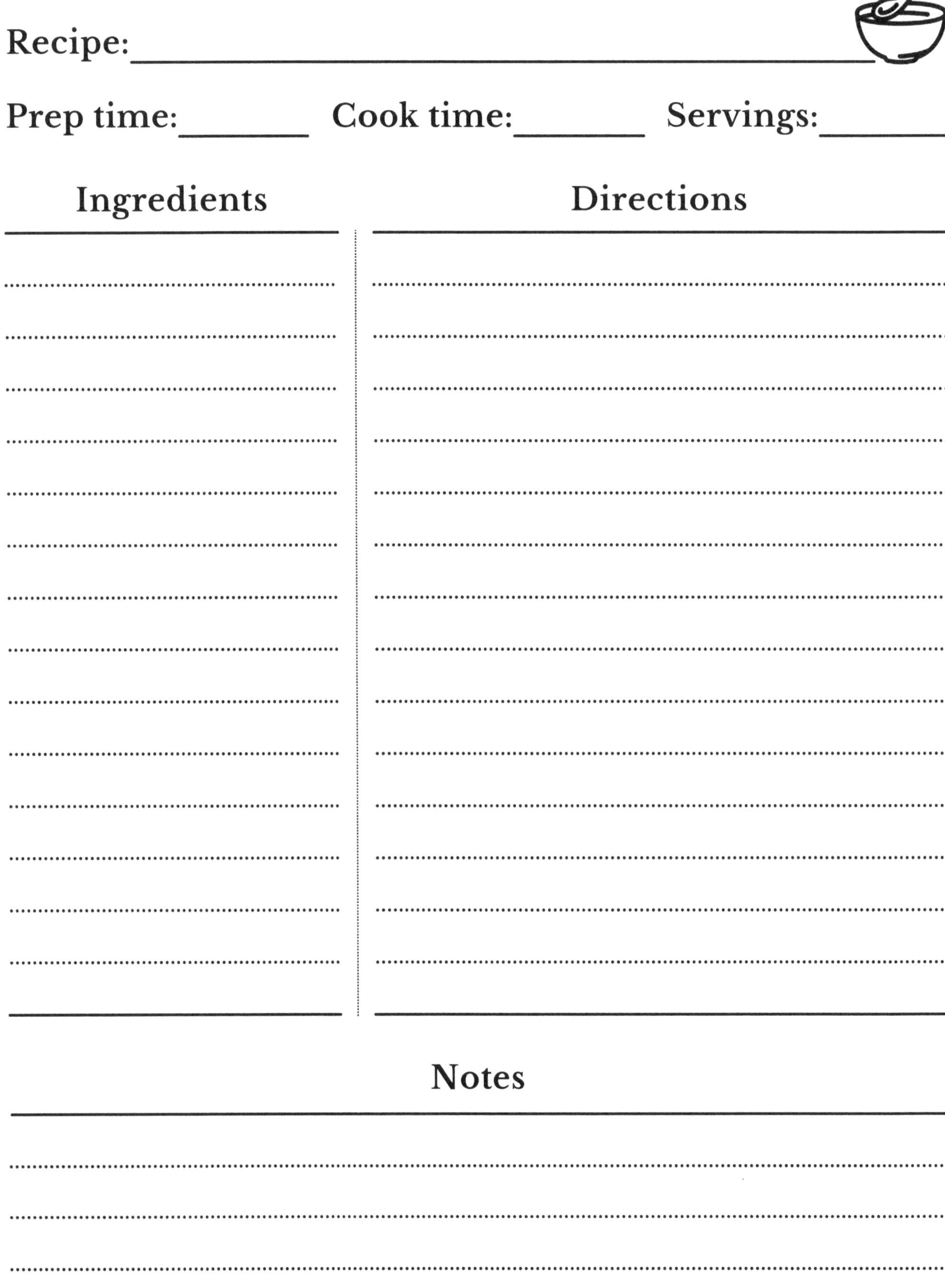

Recipe:____

Prep time:________   Cook time:________   Servings:________

Ingredients

Directions

Notes

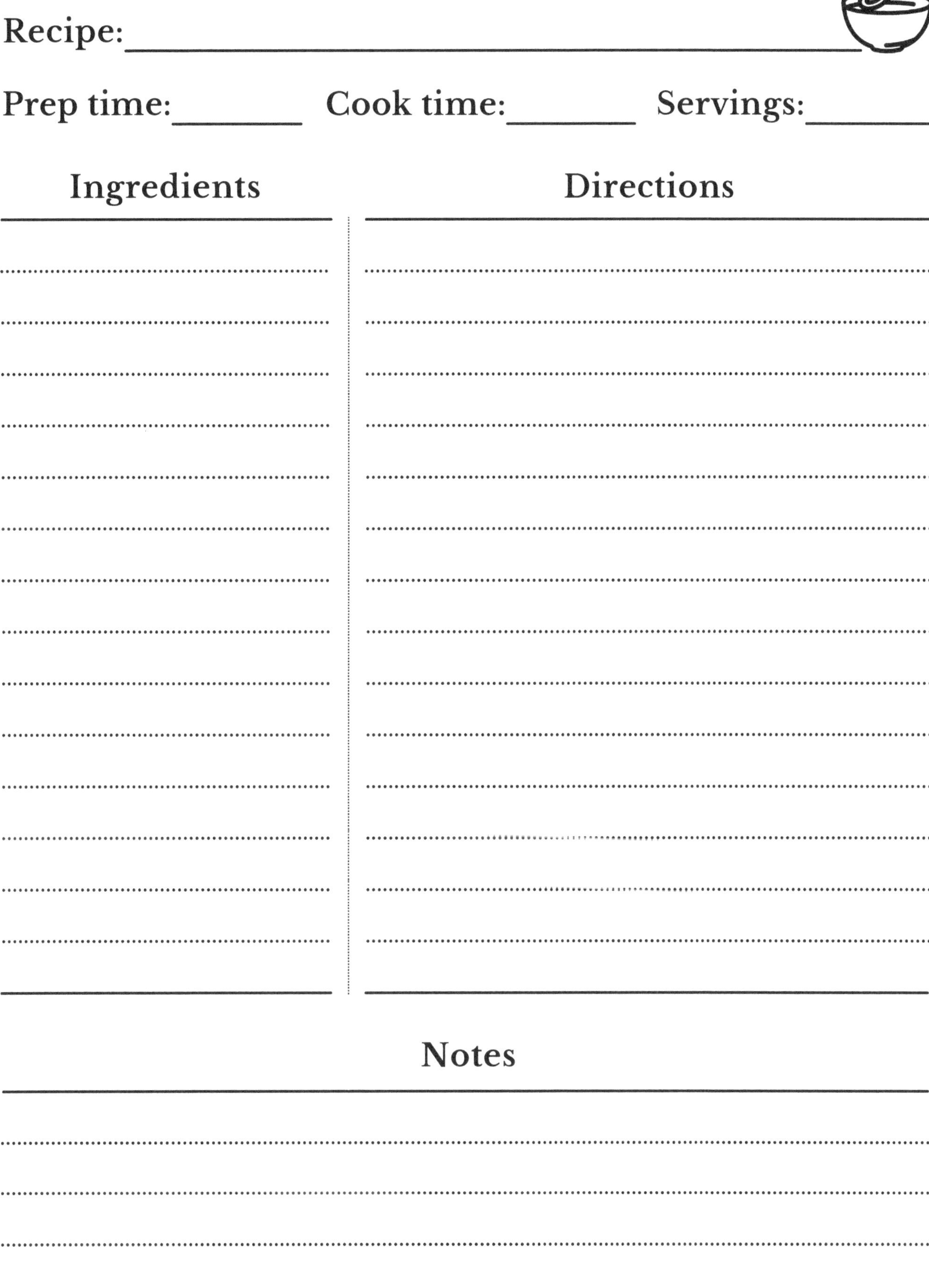

Recipe:____

Prep time:________   Cook time:________   Servings:________

Ingredients

Directions

Notes

Recipe:____ 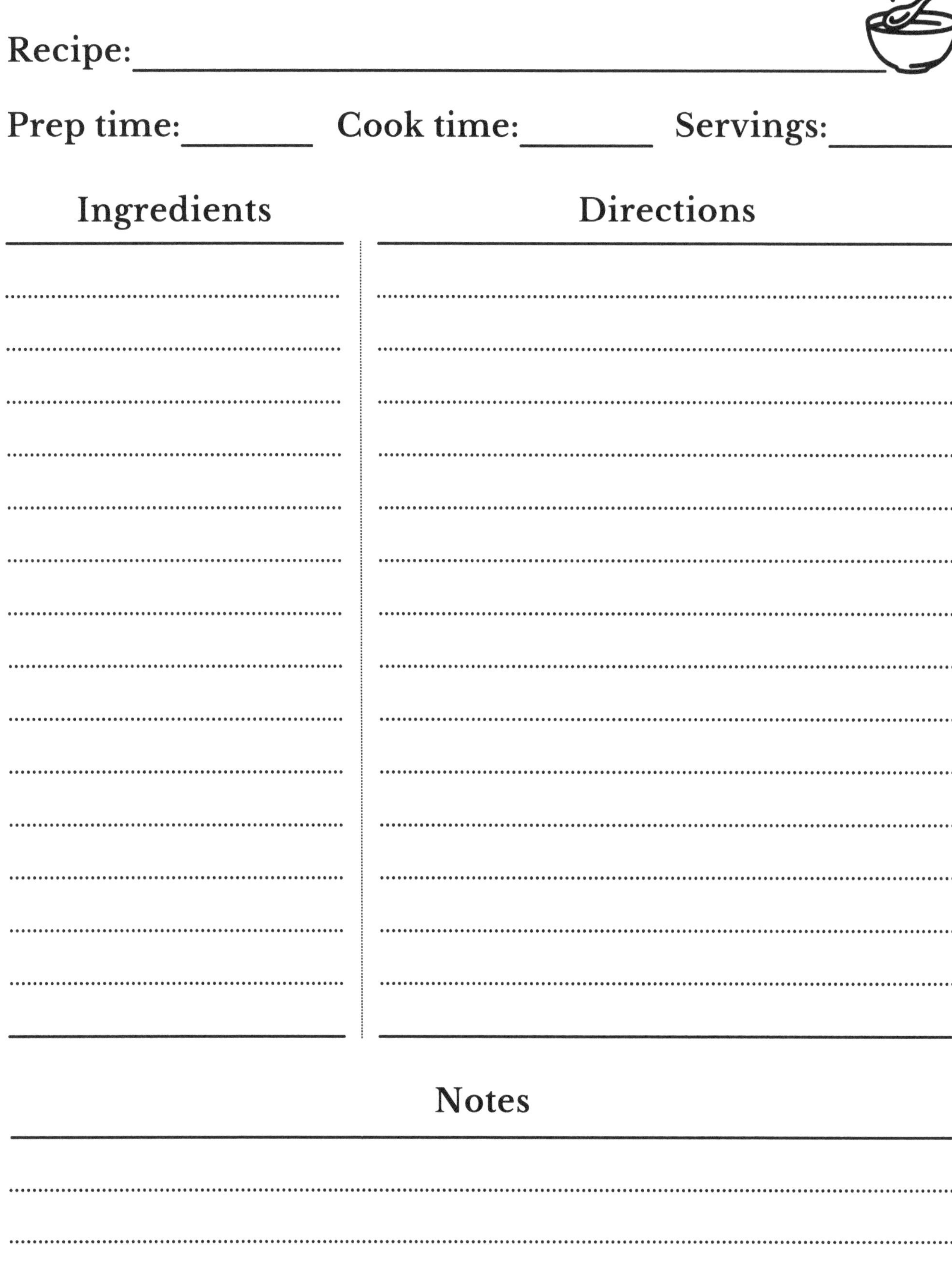

Prep time:________   Cook time:________   Servings:________

Ingredients

Directions

Notes

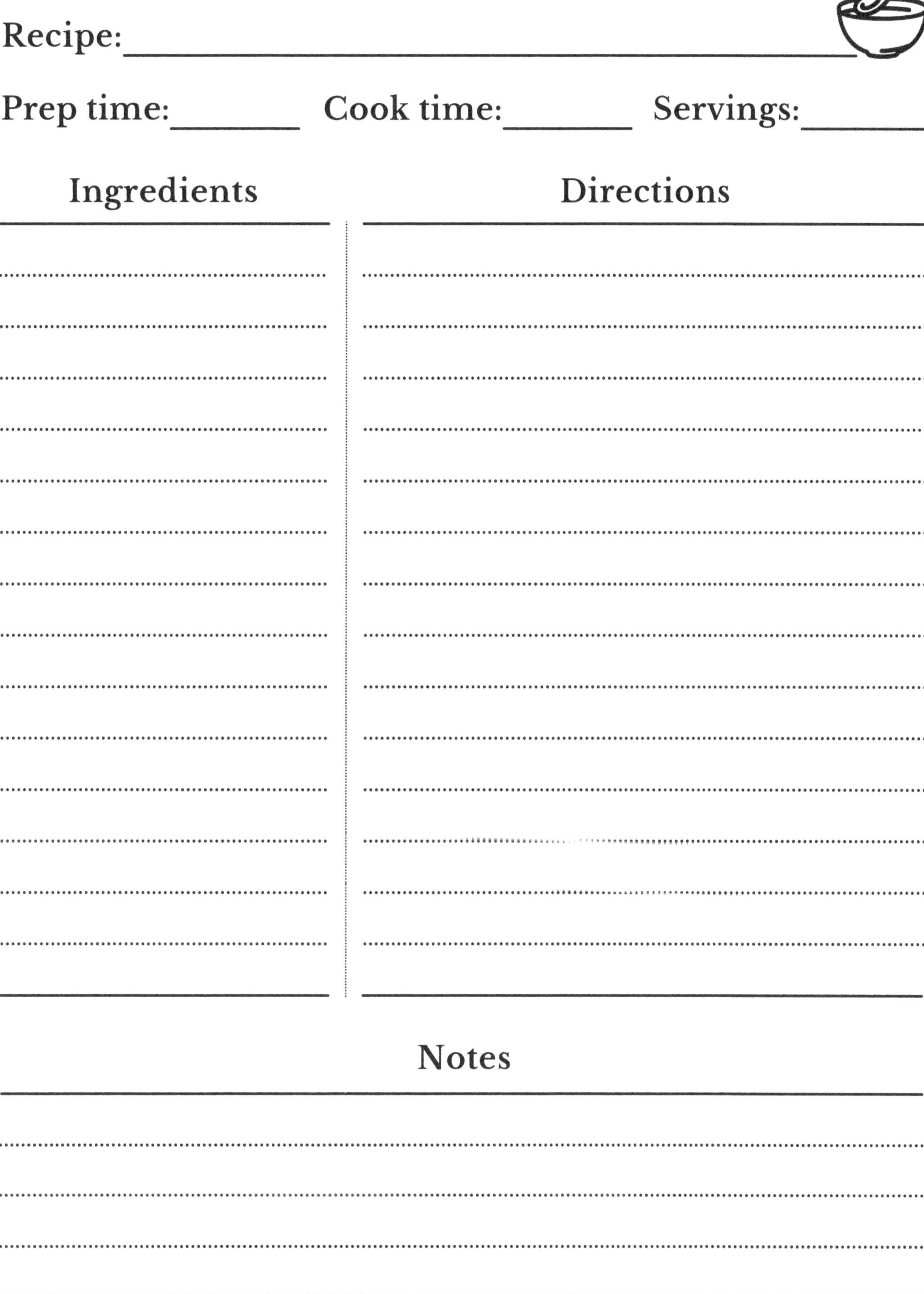

Recipe:_______________________________________

Prep time:_________ Cook time:_________ Servings:_________

Ingredients

Directions

Notes

Recipe:____ 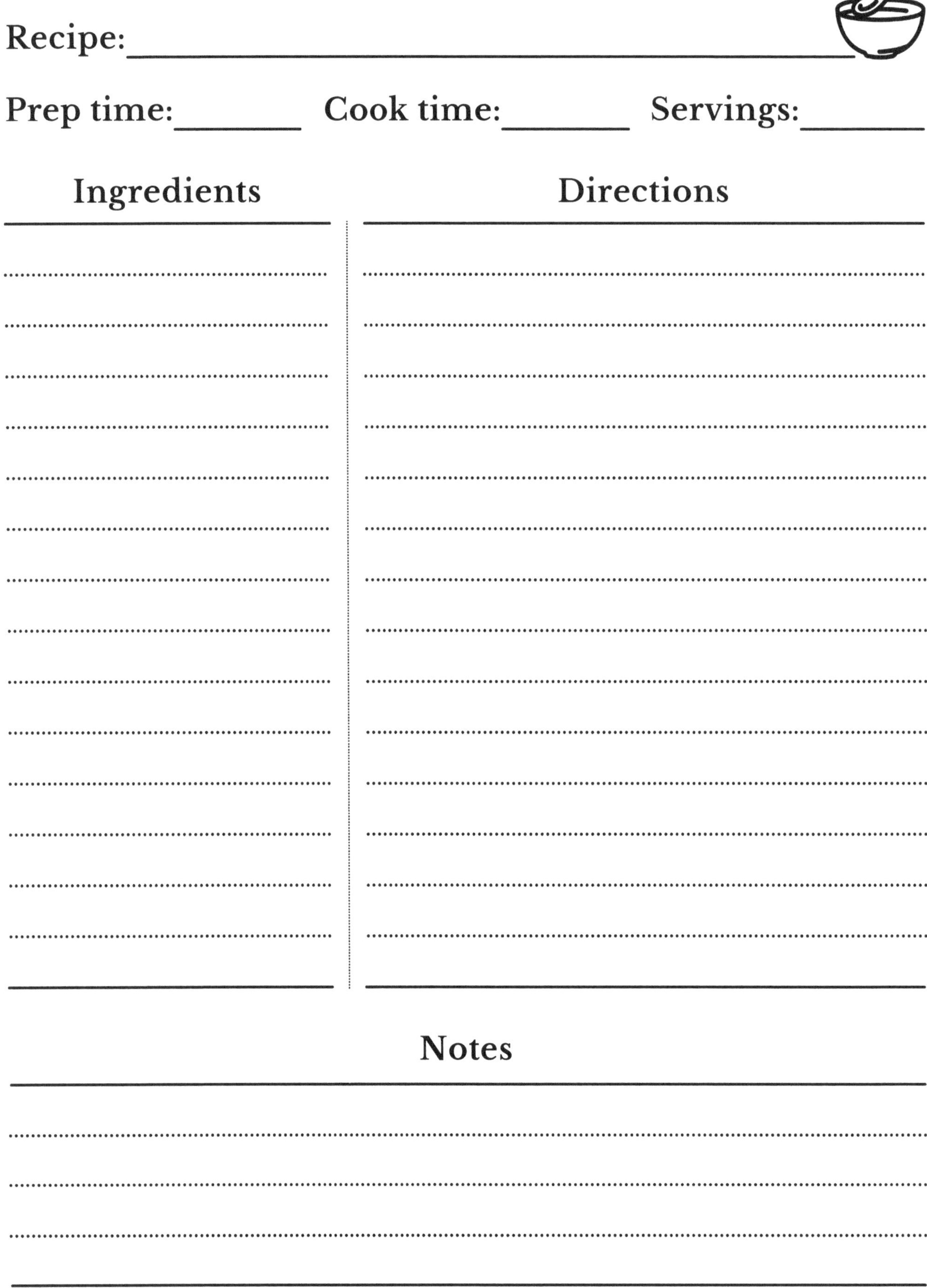

Prep time:________ Cook time:________ Servings:________

Ingredients

Directions

Notes

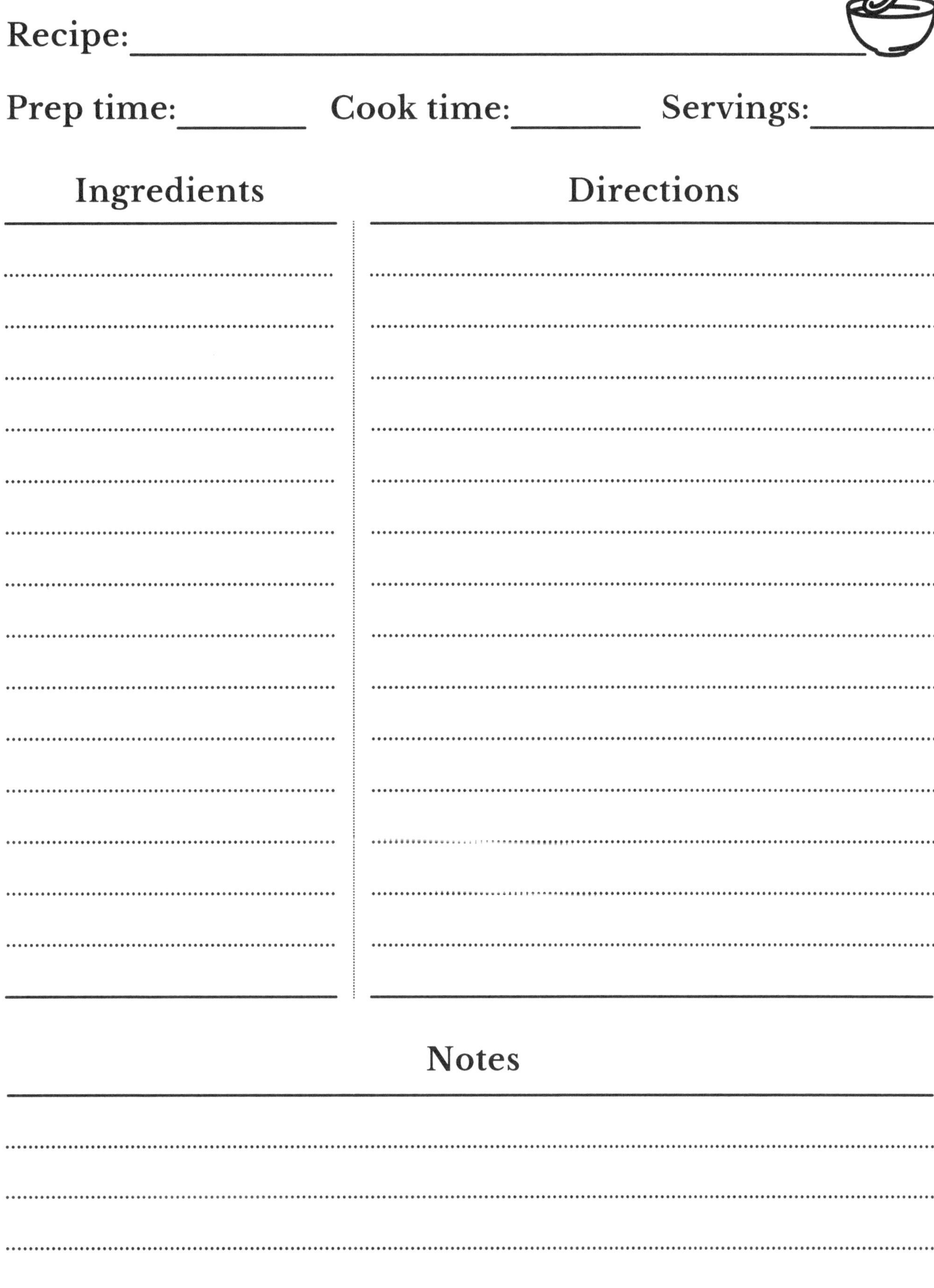

Recipe:____

Prep time:________ Cook time:________ Servings:________

Ingredients

Directions

Notes

Recipe:____ 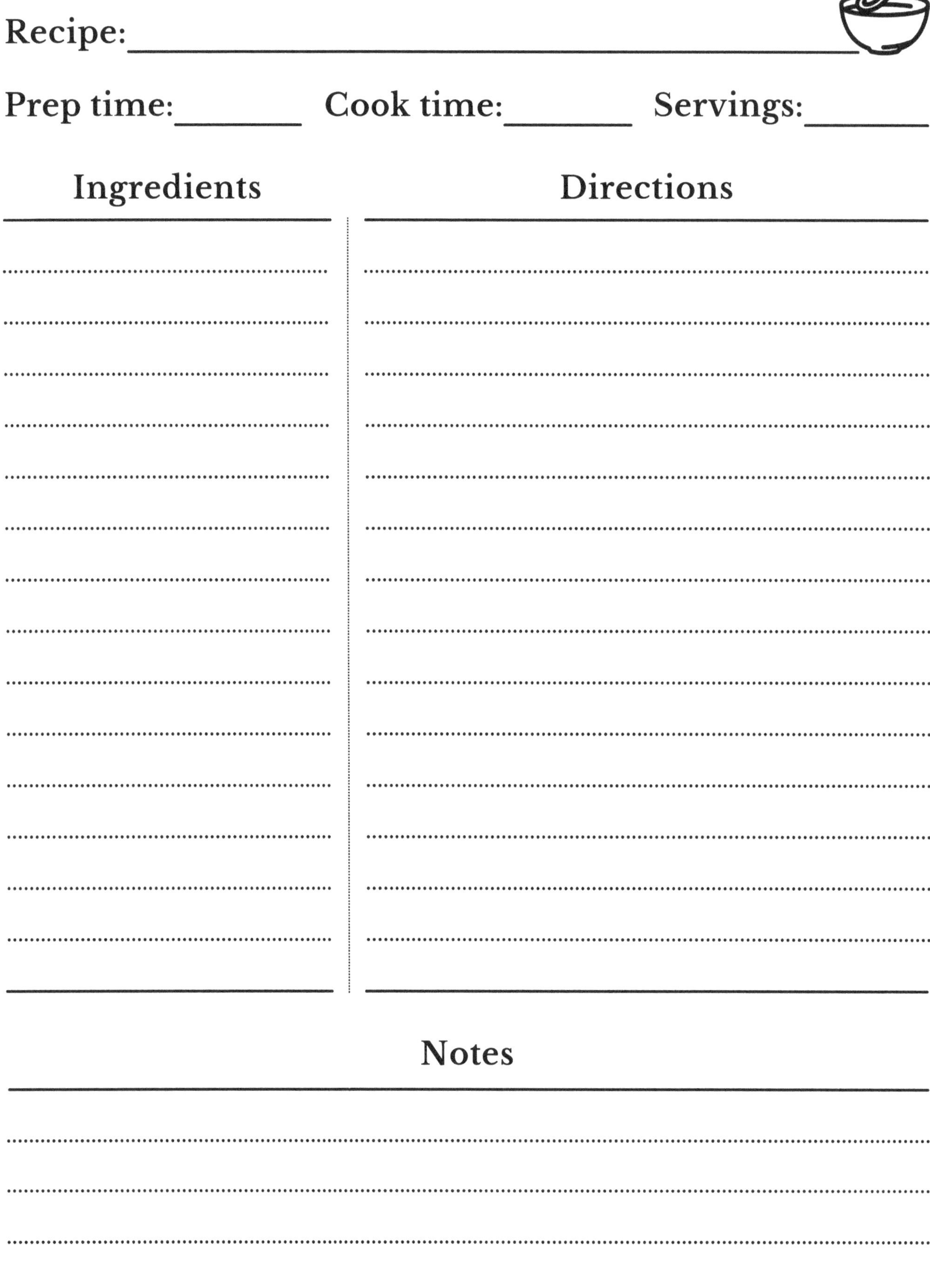

Prep time:_______   Cook time:_______   Servings:_______

Ingredients	Directions

Notes

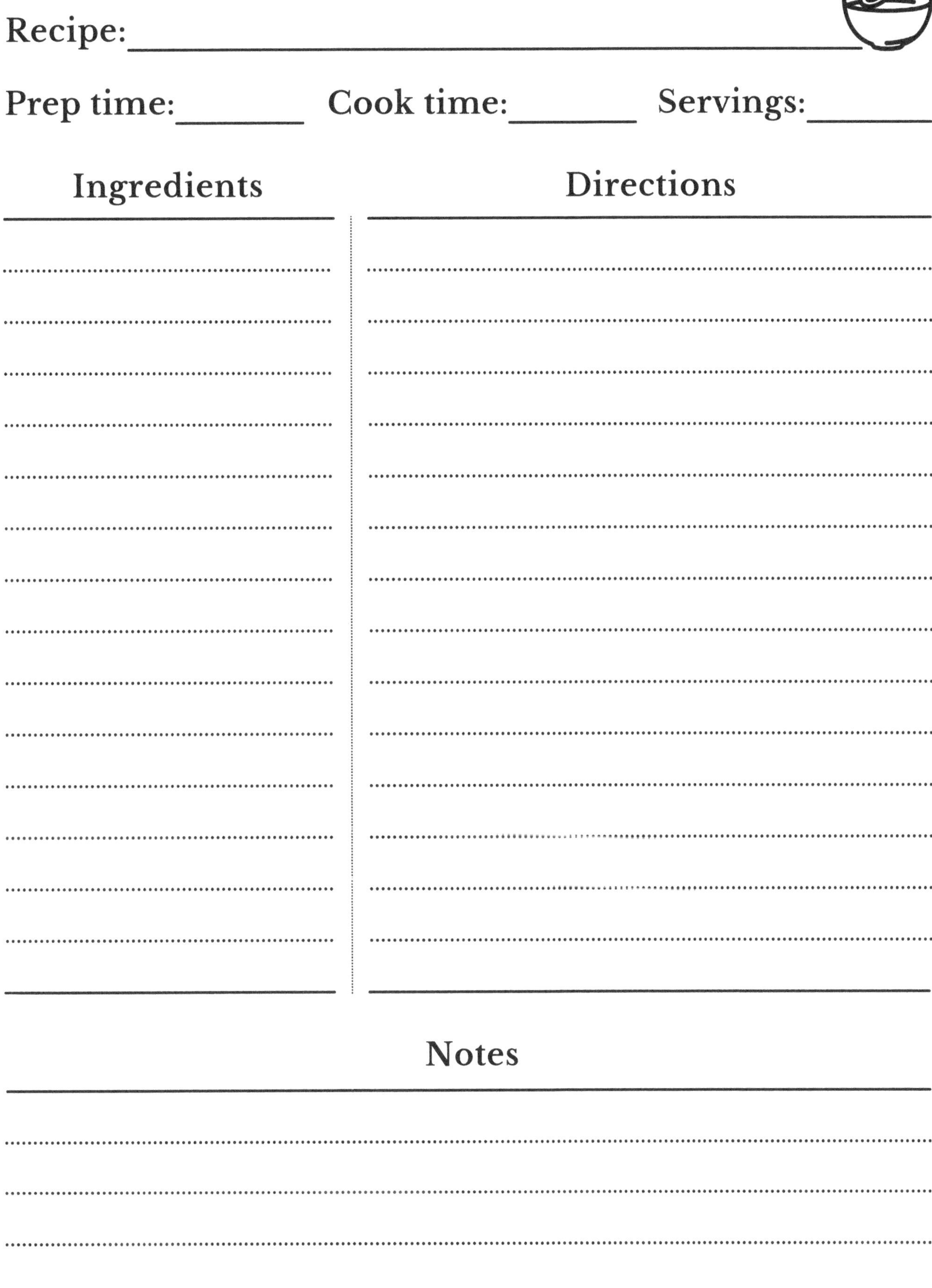

Recipe:____

Prep time:________   Cook time:________   Servings:________

Ingredients

Directions

Notes

Recipe:____

Prep time:_______ Cook time:_______ Servings:_______

Ingredients

Directions

Notes

Recipe:____ 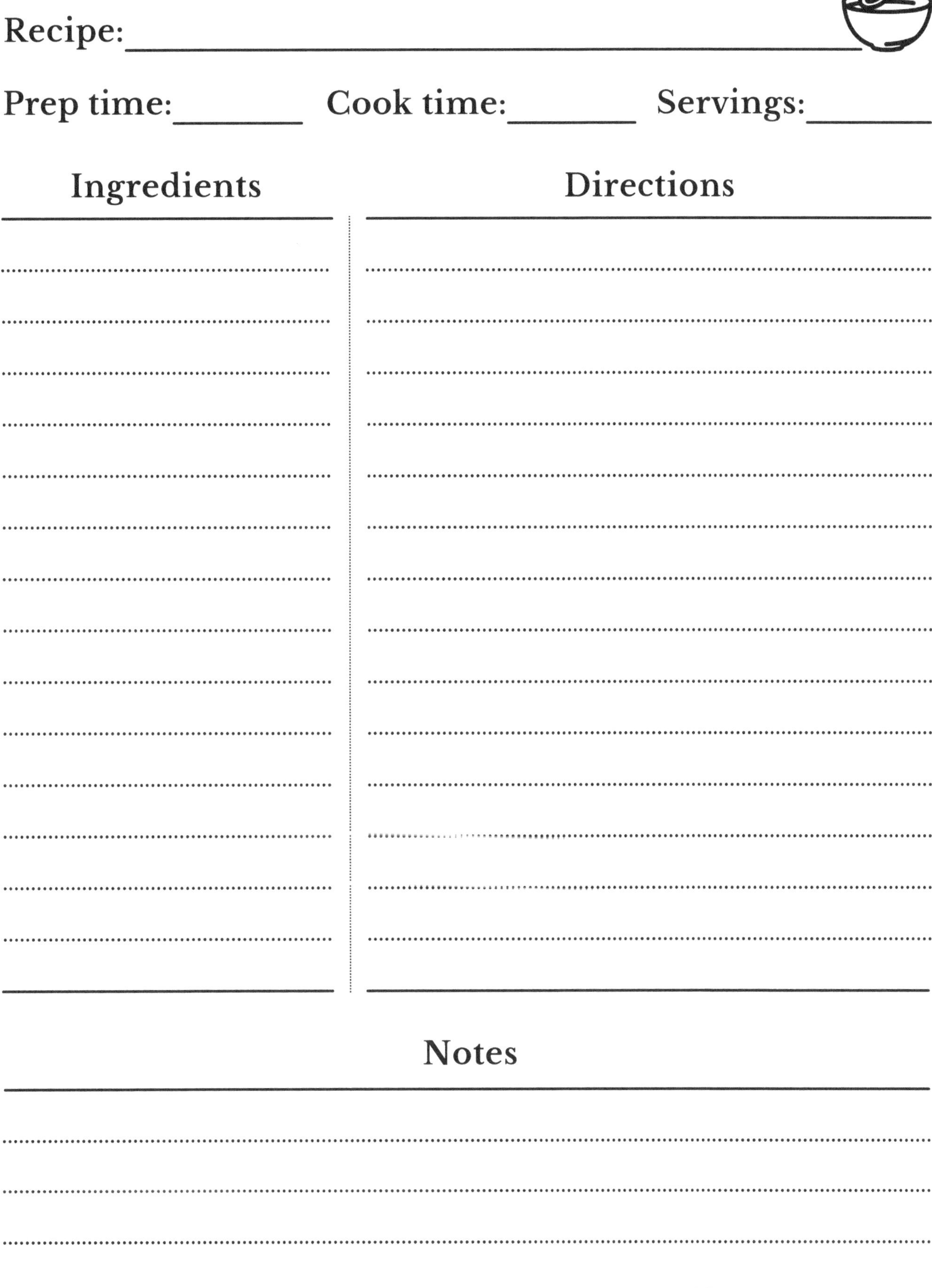

Prep time:________   Cook time:________   Servings:________

Ingredients

Directions

Notes

Recipe:____ 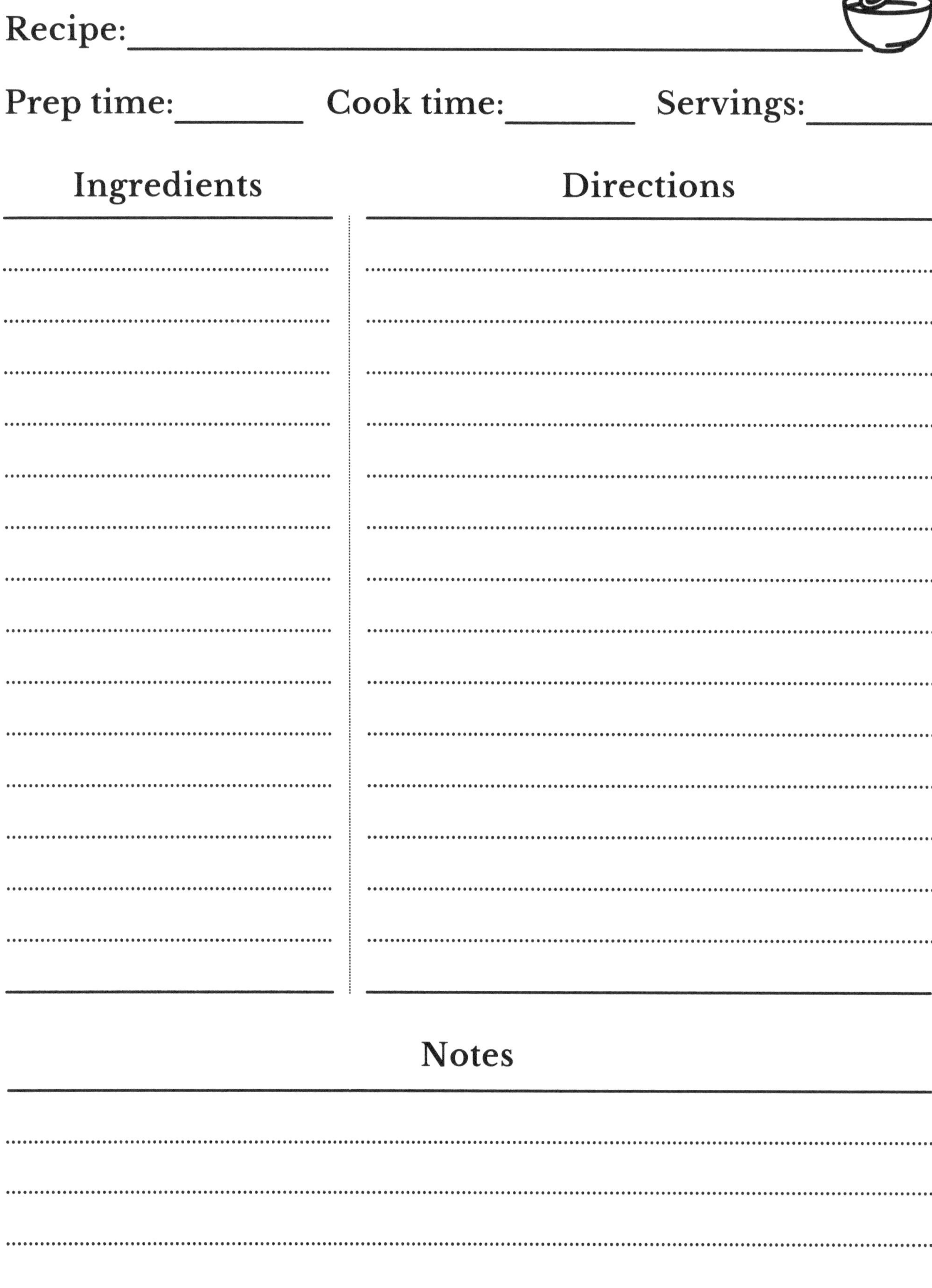

Prep time:_______ Cook time:_______ Servings:_______

Ingredients	Directions

Notes

Recipe:

Prep time:______ Cook time:______ Servings:______

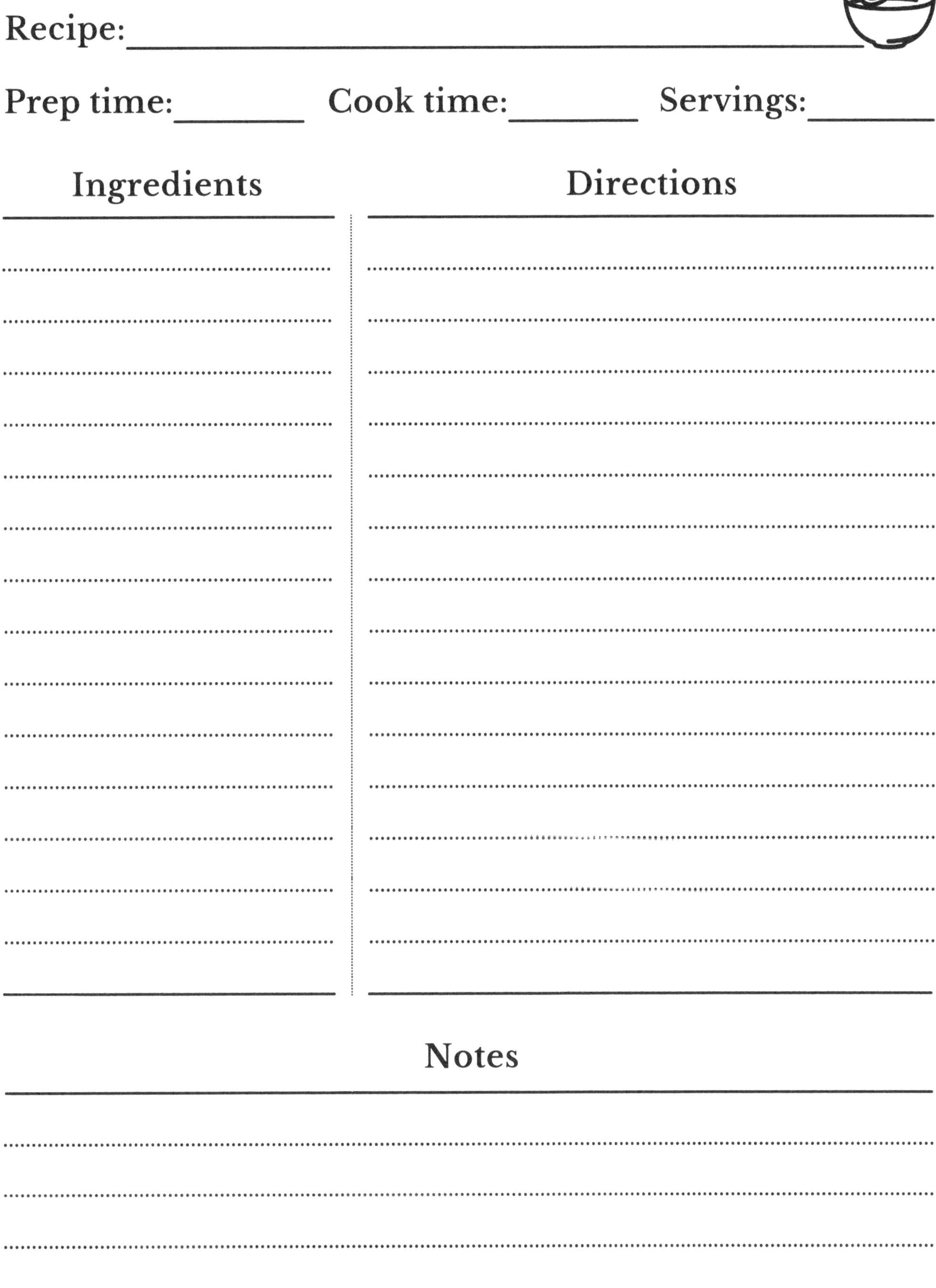

Ingredients

Directions

Notes

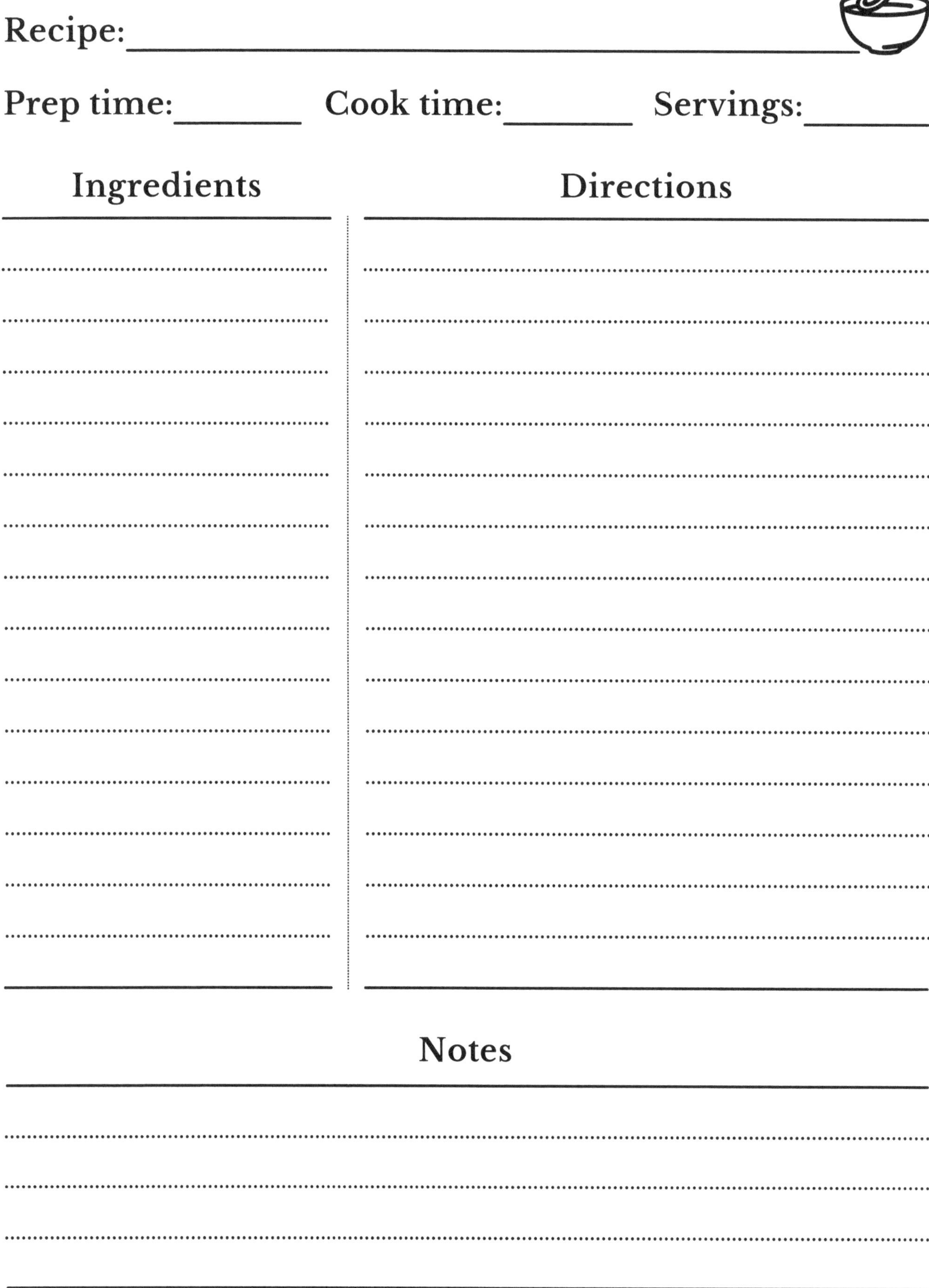

Recipe:_______________________________________

Prep time:_______   Cook time:_______   Servings:_______

Ingredients

Directions

Notes

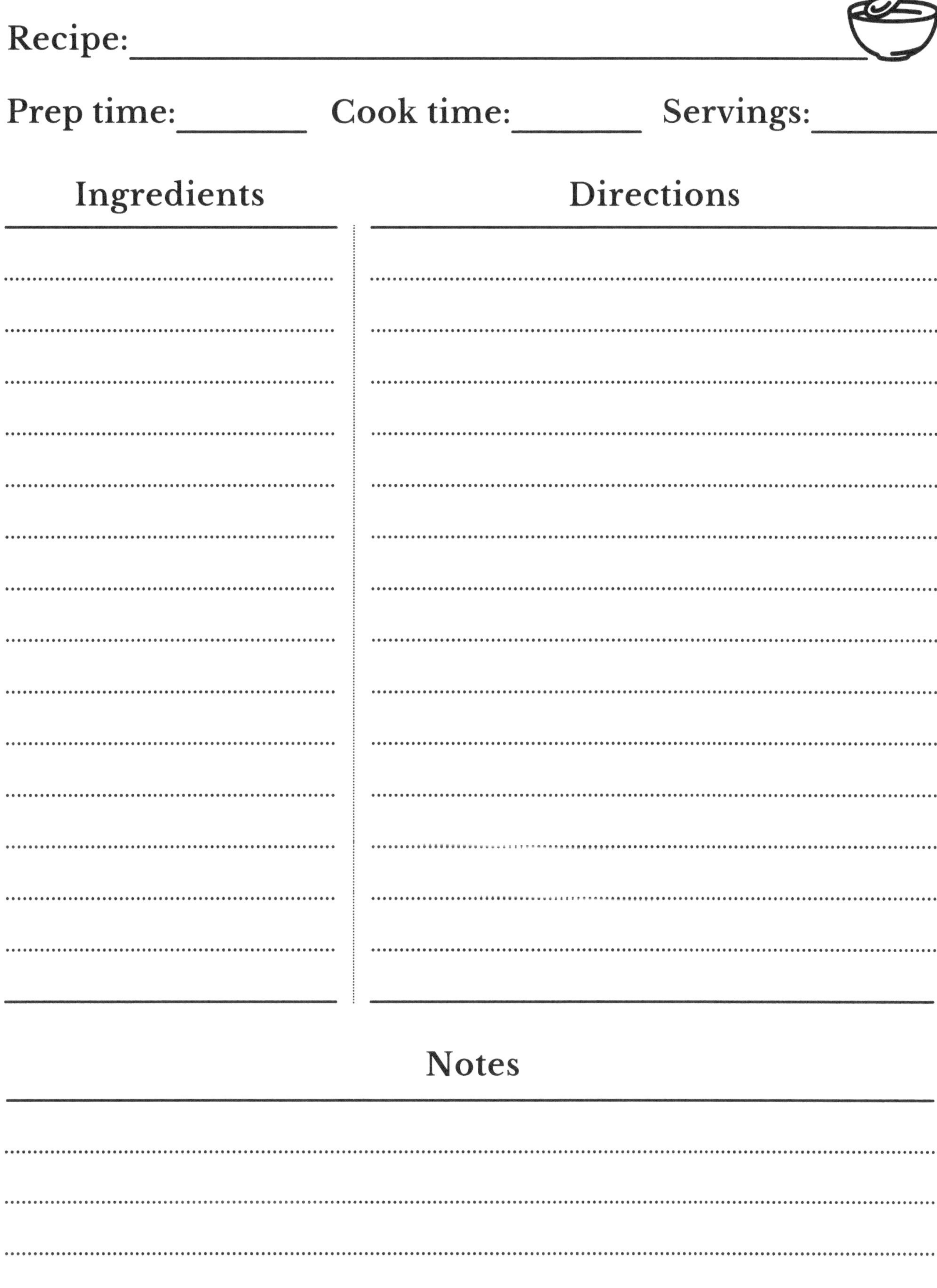

Recipe:

Prep time: _______ **Cook time:** _______ **Servings:** _______

Ingredients

Directions

Notes

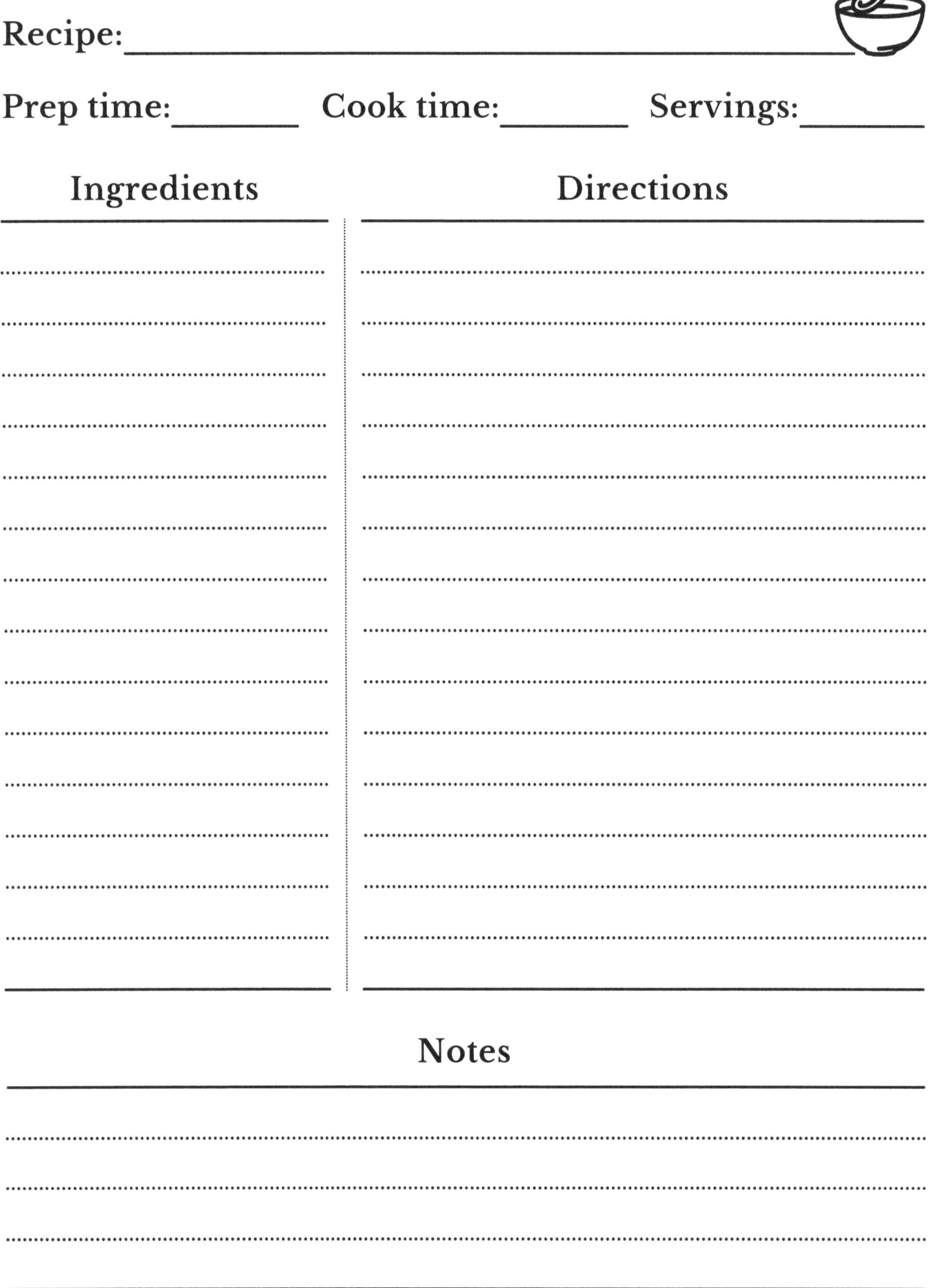

Recipe:

Prep time:______ Cook time:______ Servings:______

Ingredients

Directions

Notes

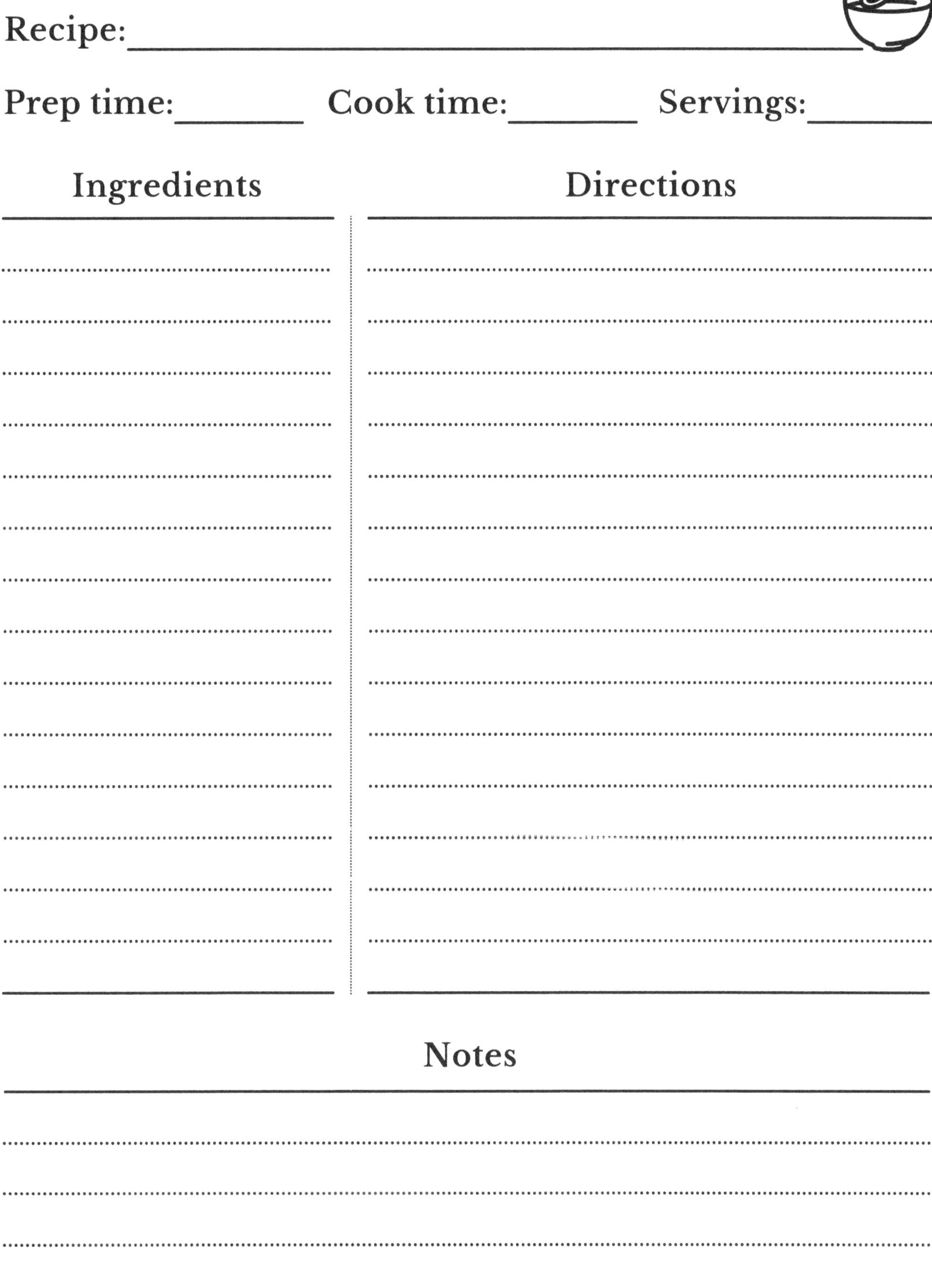

Recipe:____

Prep time:________ Cook time:________ Servings:________

Ingredients	Directions

Notes

Recipe:____

Prep time:________ Cook time:________ Servings:________

Ingredients

Directions

Notes

Recipe:

Prep time: ______   **Cook time:** ______   **Servings:** ______

Ingredients

Directions

Notes

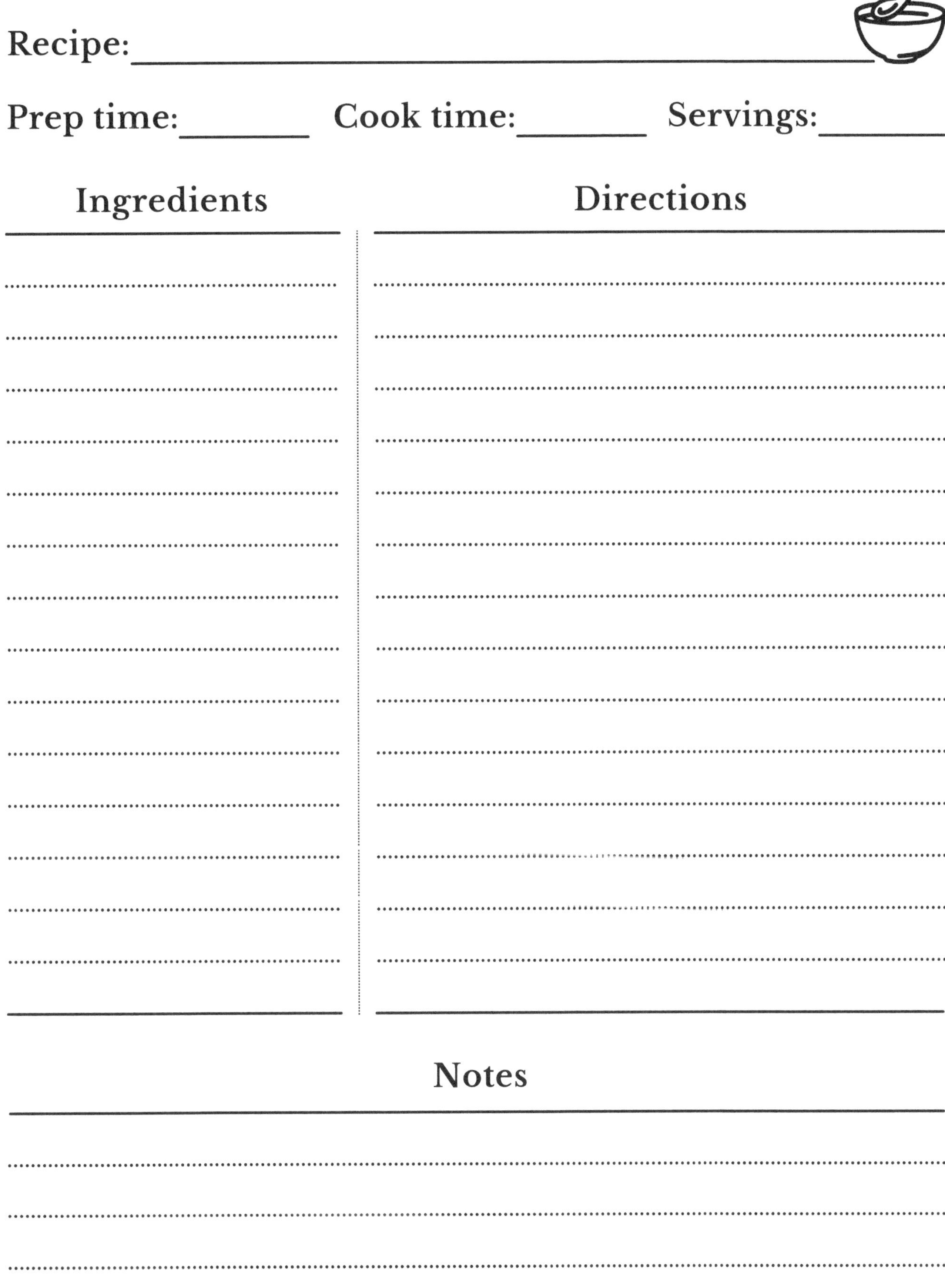

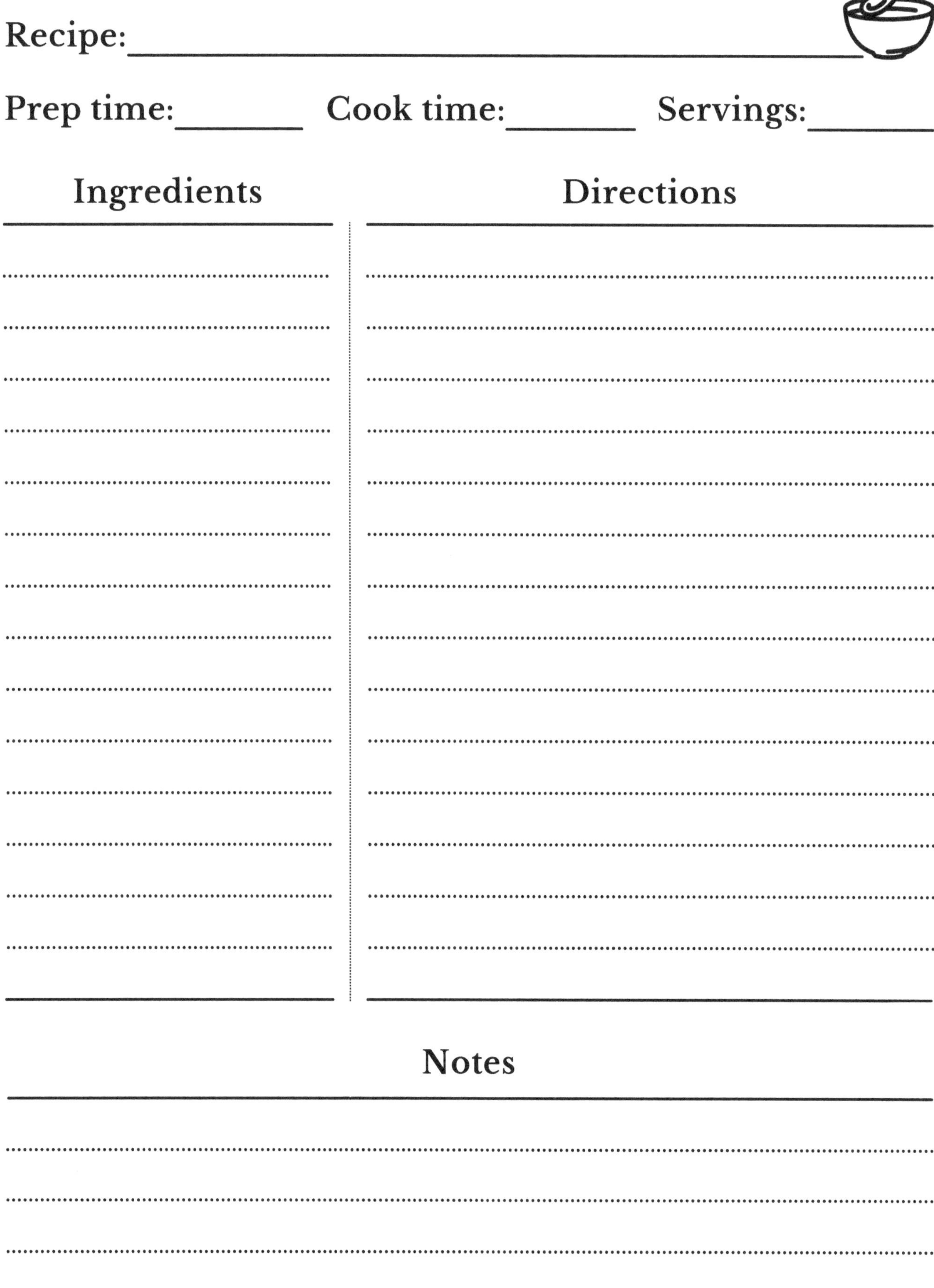

Recipe:____

Prep time:________ Cook time:________ Servings:________

Ingredients

Directions

Notes

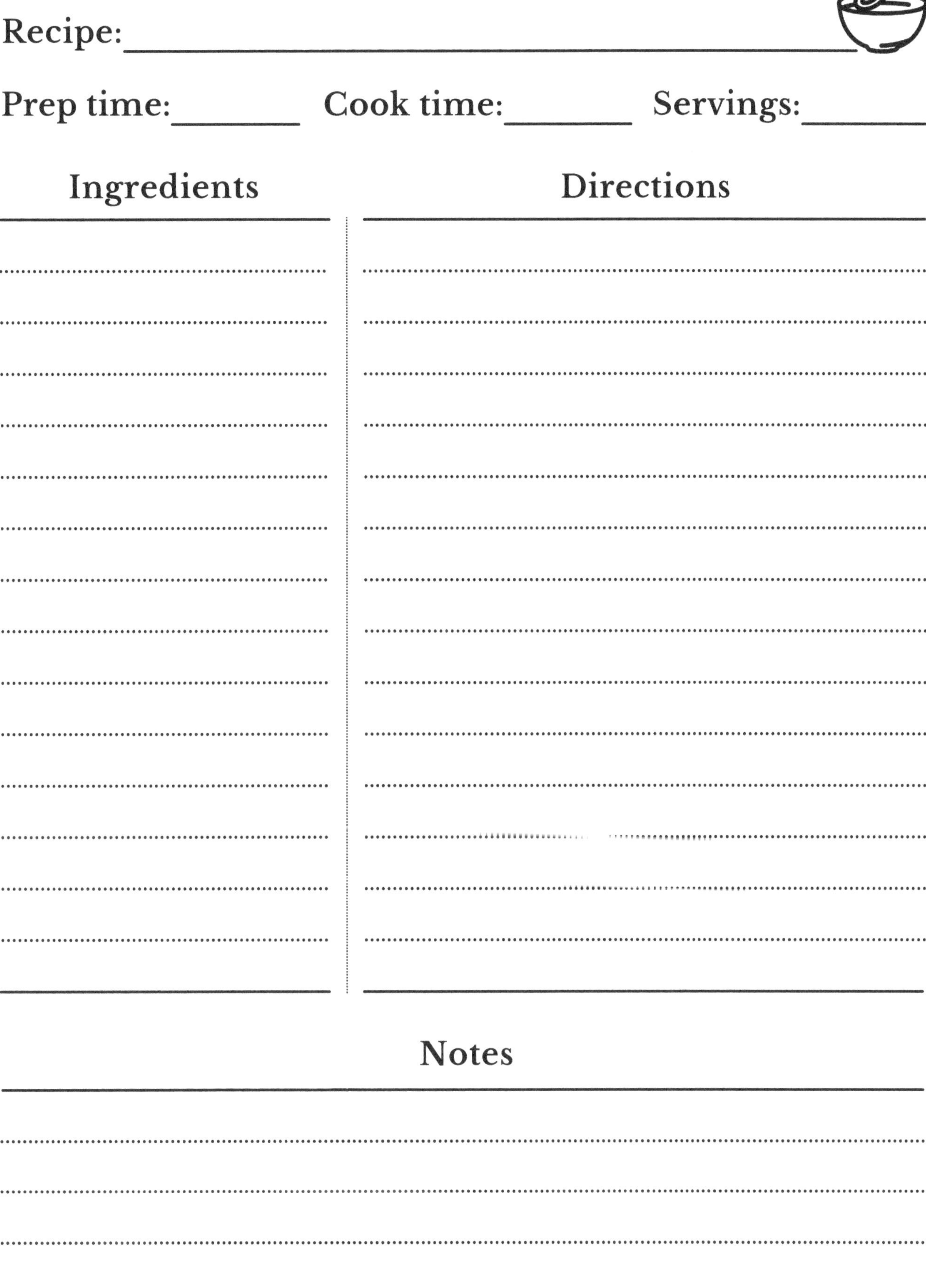

Recipe:

Prep time: _______ Cook time: _______ Servings: _______

Ingredients

Directions

Notes

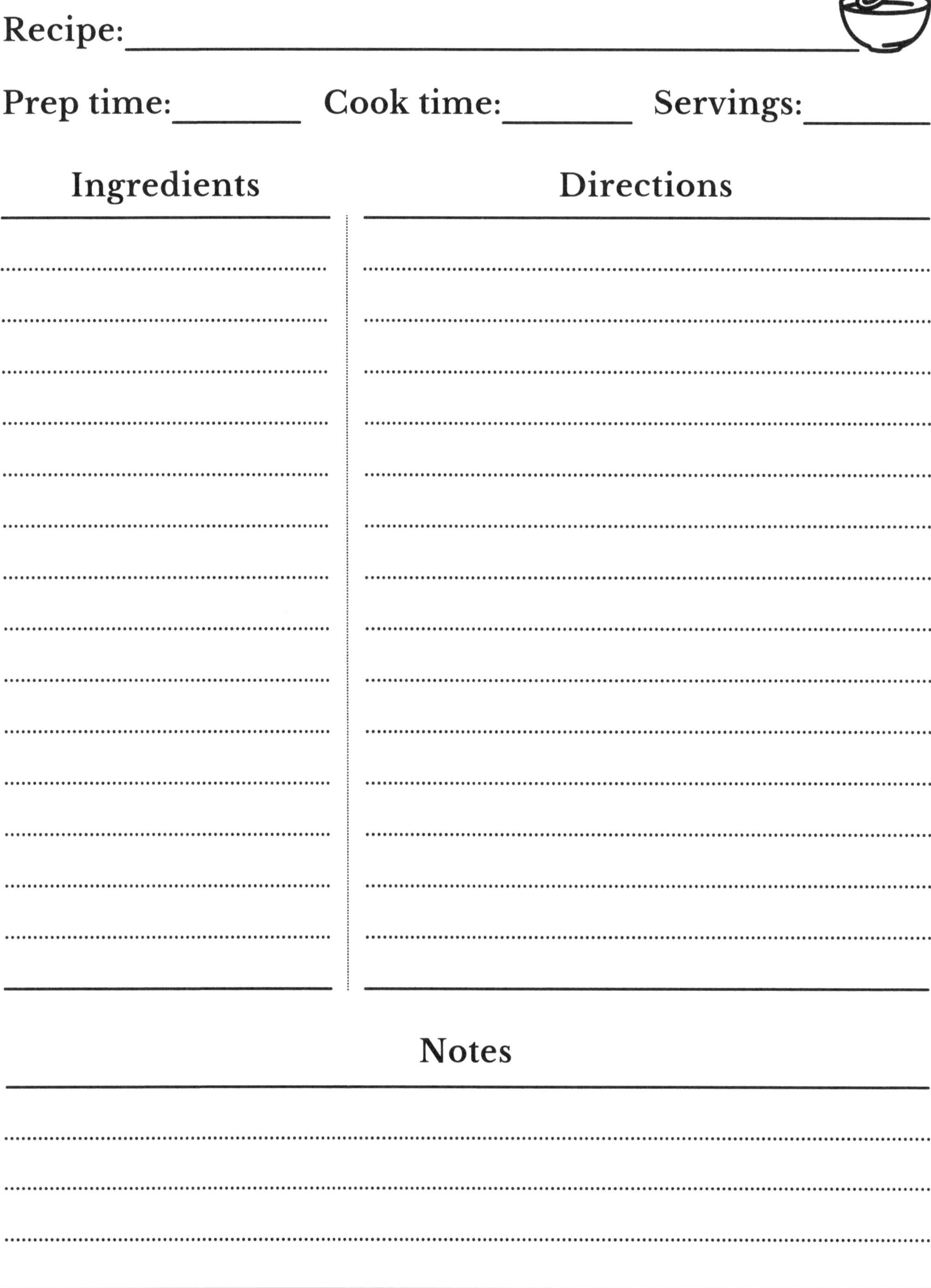

Recipe:____

Prep time:_______   Cook time:_______   Servings:_______

Ingredients

Directions

Notes

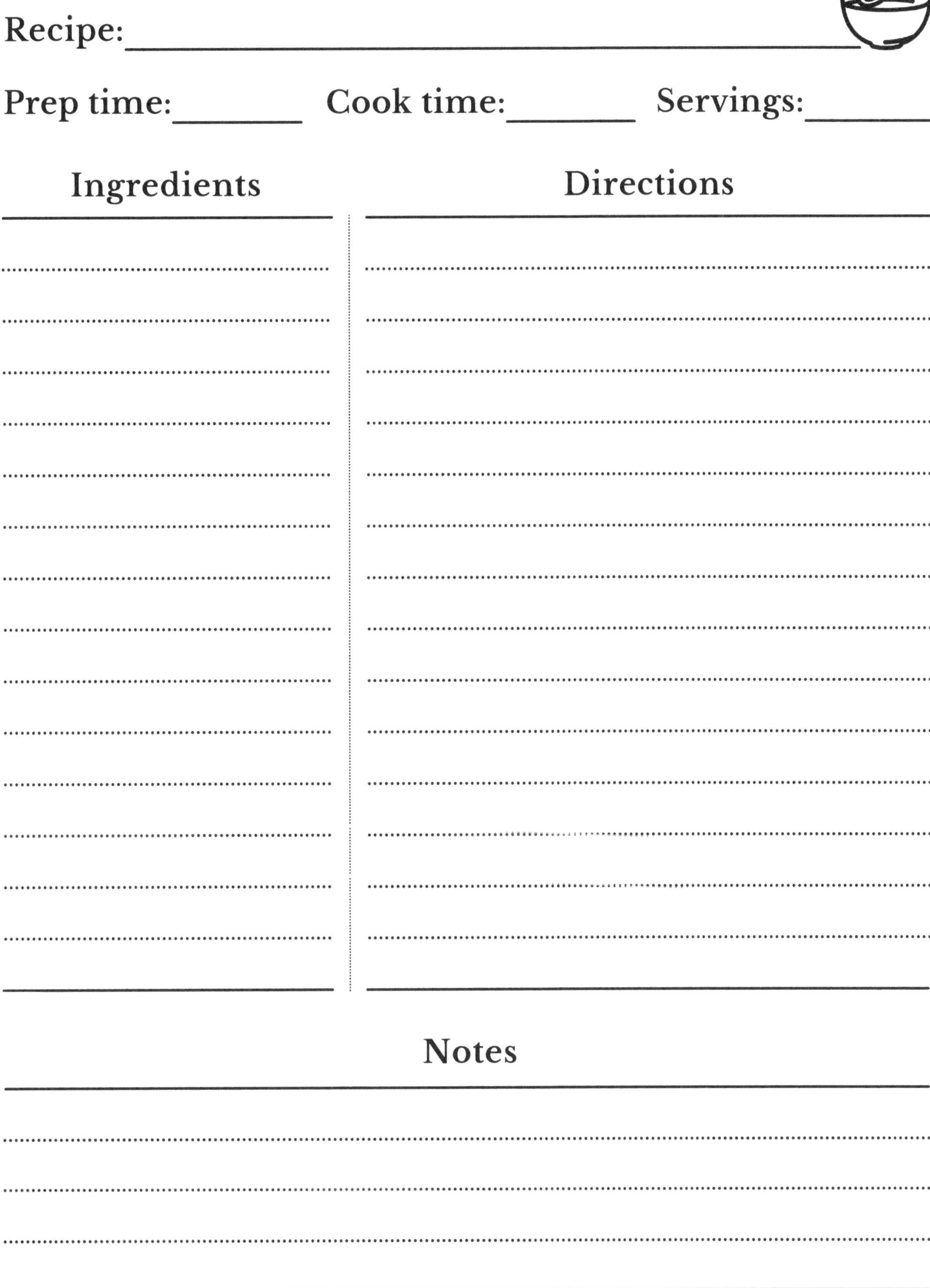

Recipe:____

Prep time:________ Cook time:________ Servings:________

Ingredients

Directions

Notes

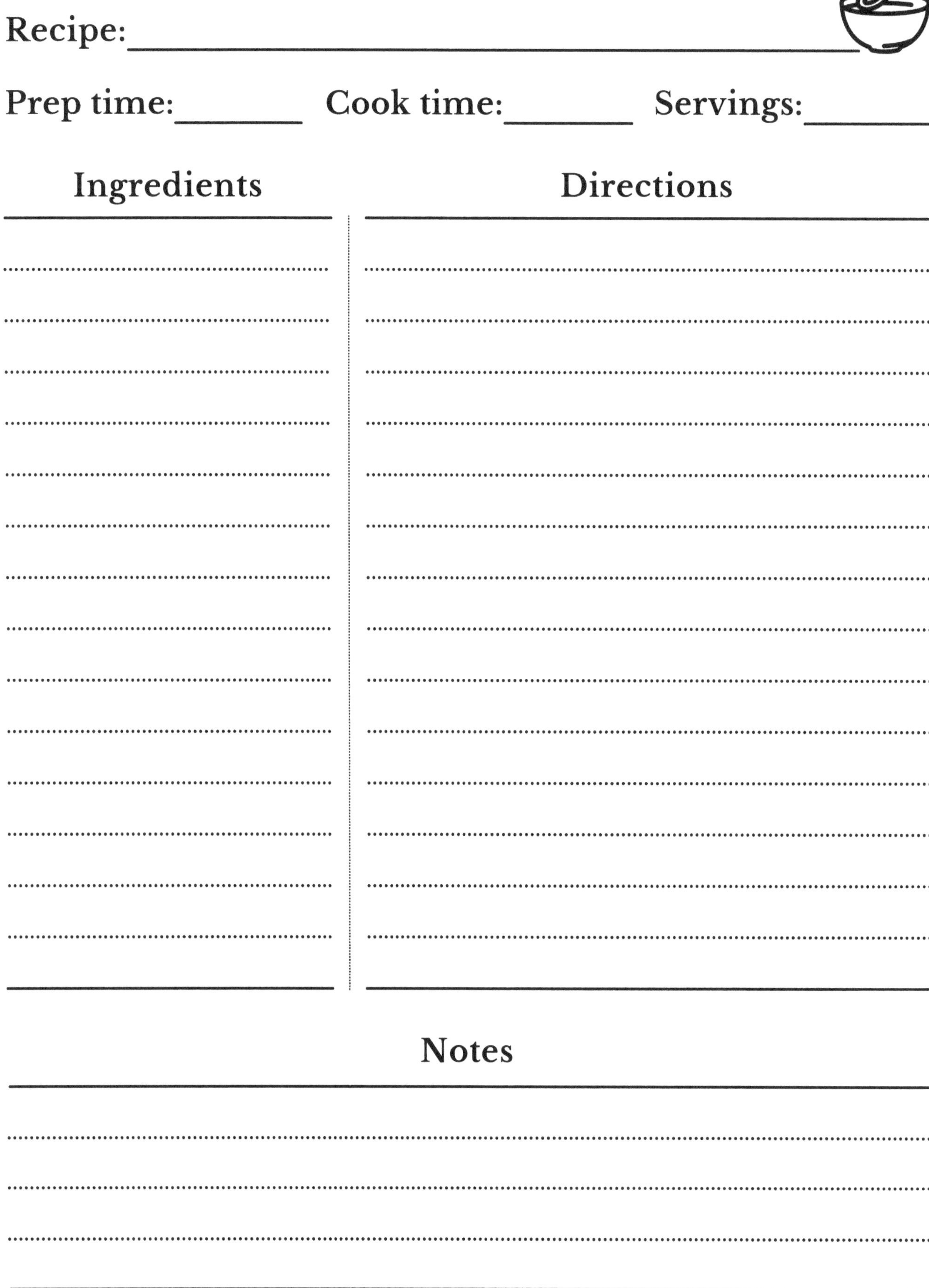

Recipe:

Prep time: Cook time: Servings:

Ingredients

Directions

Notes

Recipe:_______________________________________

Prep time:_______   Cook time:_______   Servings:_______

Ingredients

Directions

Notes

Recipe: _________________________________

Prep time: _______ **Cook time:** _______ **Servings:** _______

Ingredients	Directions

Notes

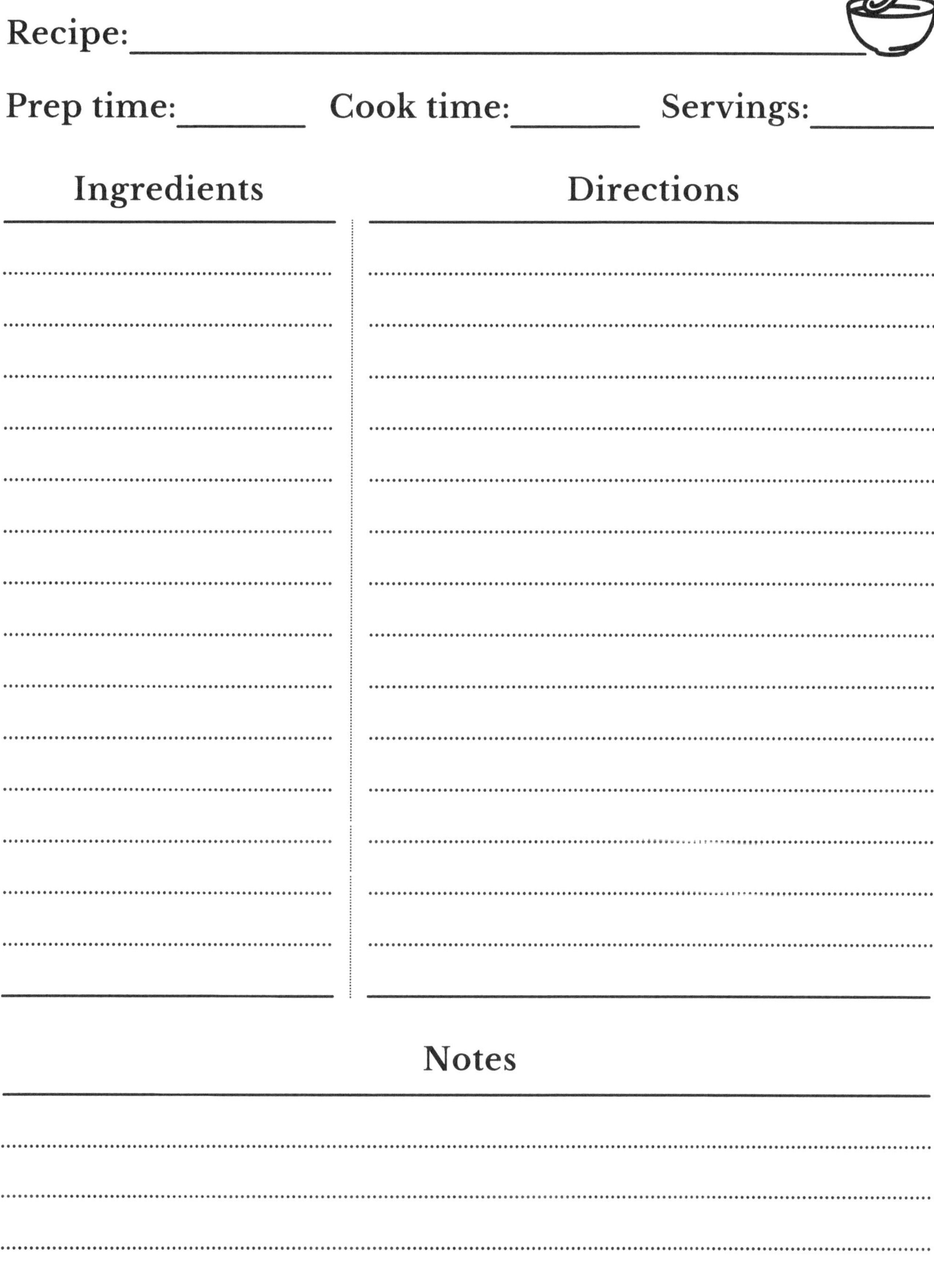

Recipe:____

Prep time:_______ Cook time:_______ Servings:_______

Ingredients

Directions

Notes

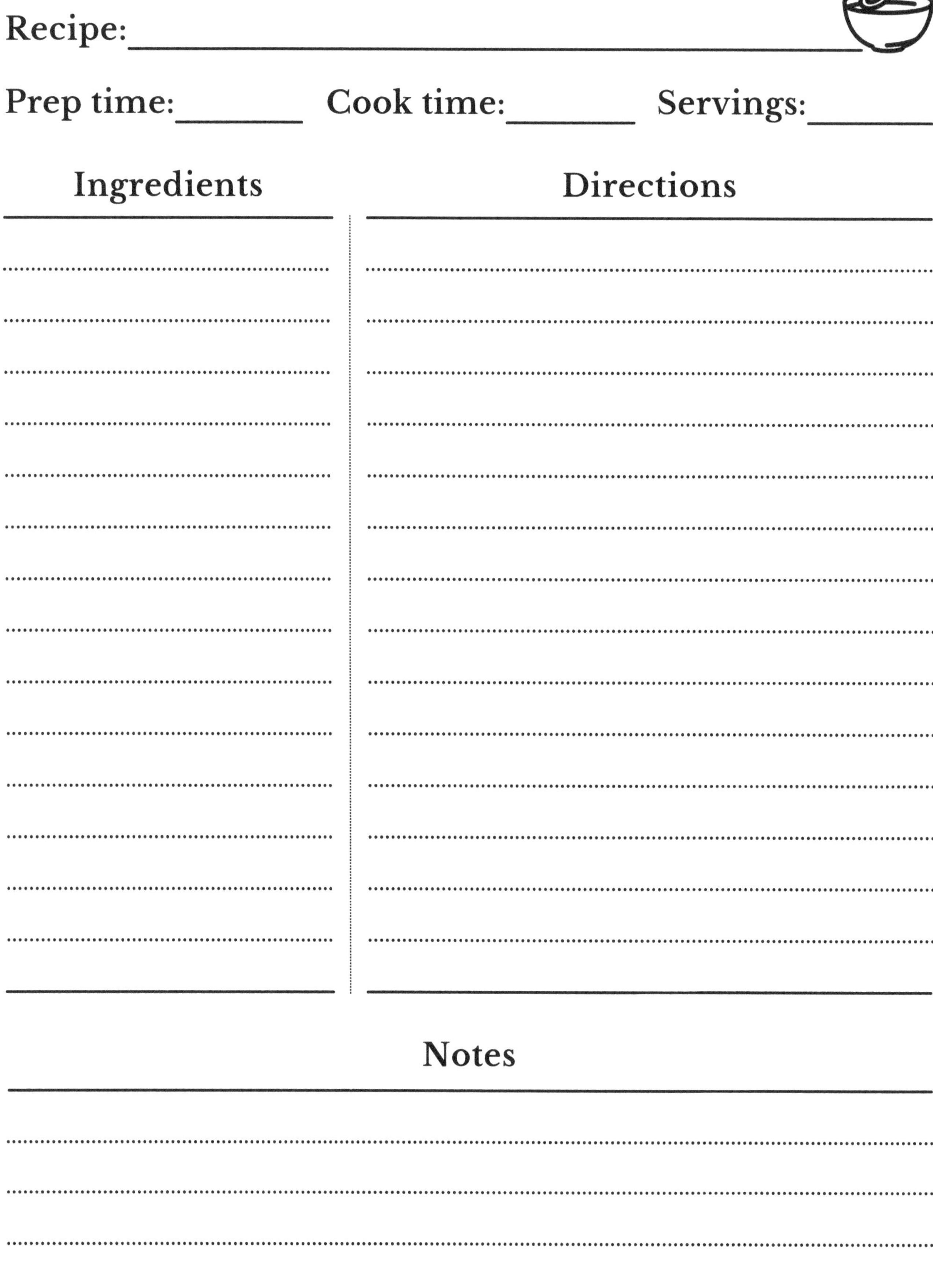

Recipe:____

Prep time:_______ Cook time:_______ Servings:_______

Ingredients

Directions

Notes

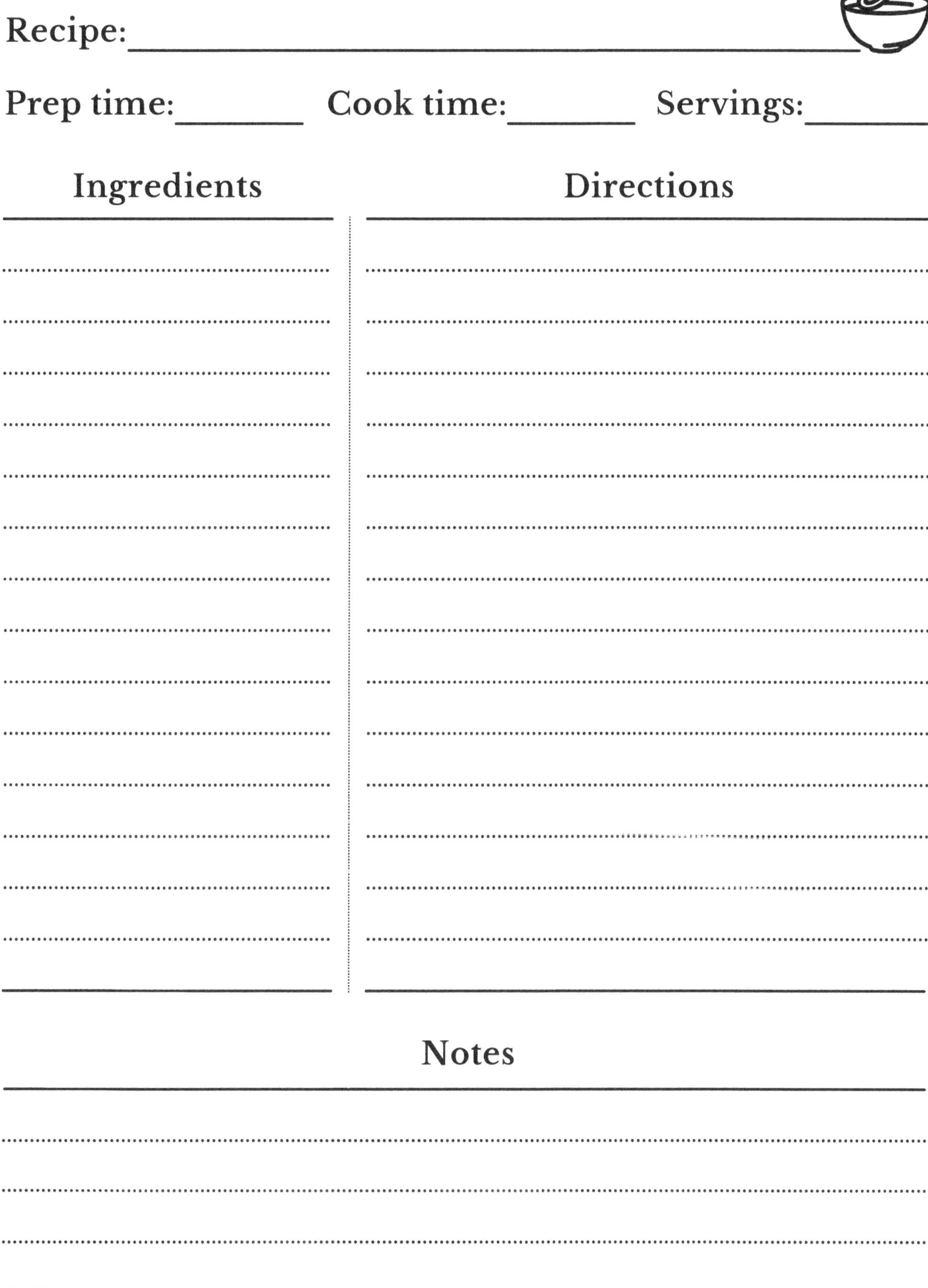

Recipe:_______________________________________

Prep time:_______ Cook time:_______ Servings:_______

Ingredients

Directions

Notes

Recipe:_______________________________________

Prep time:_______   Cook time:_______   Servings:_______

Ingredients

Directions

Notes

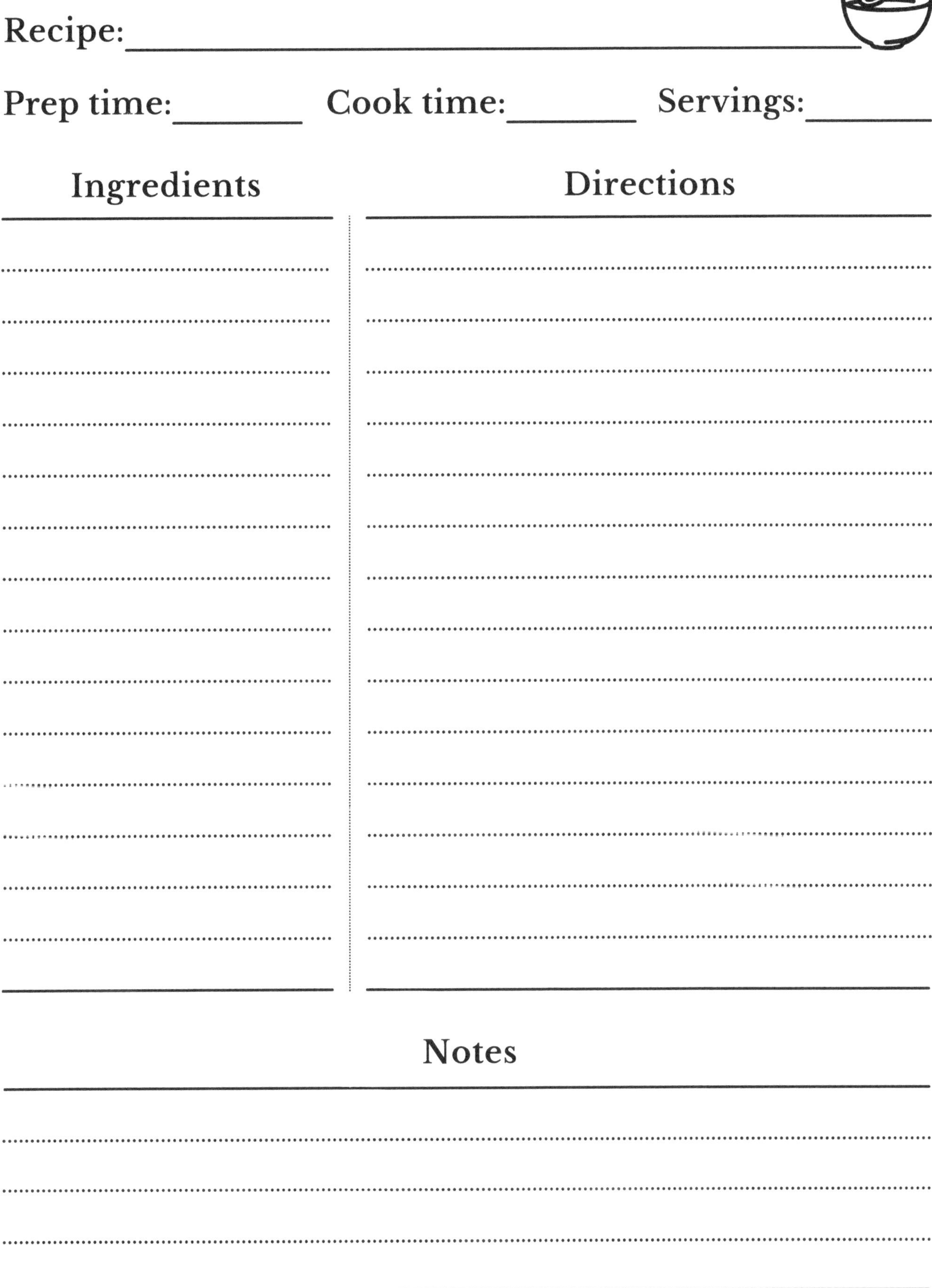

Recipe:____

Prep time:_________ Cook time:_________ Servings:_________

Ingredients

Directions

Notes

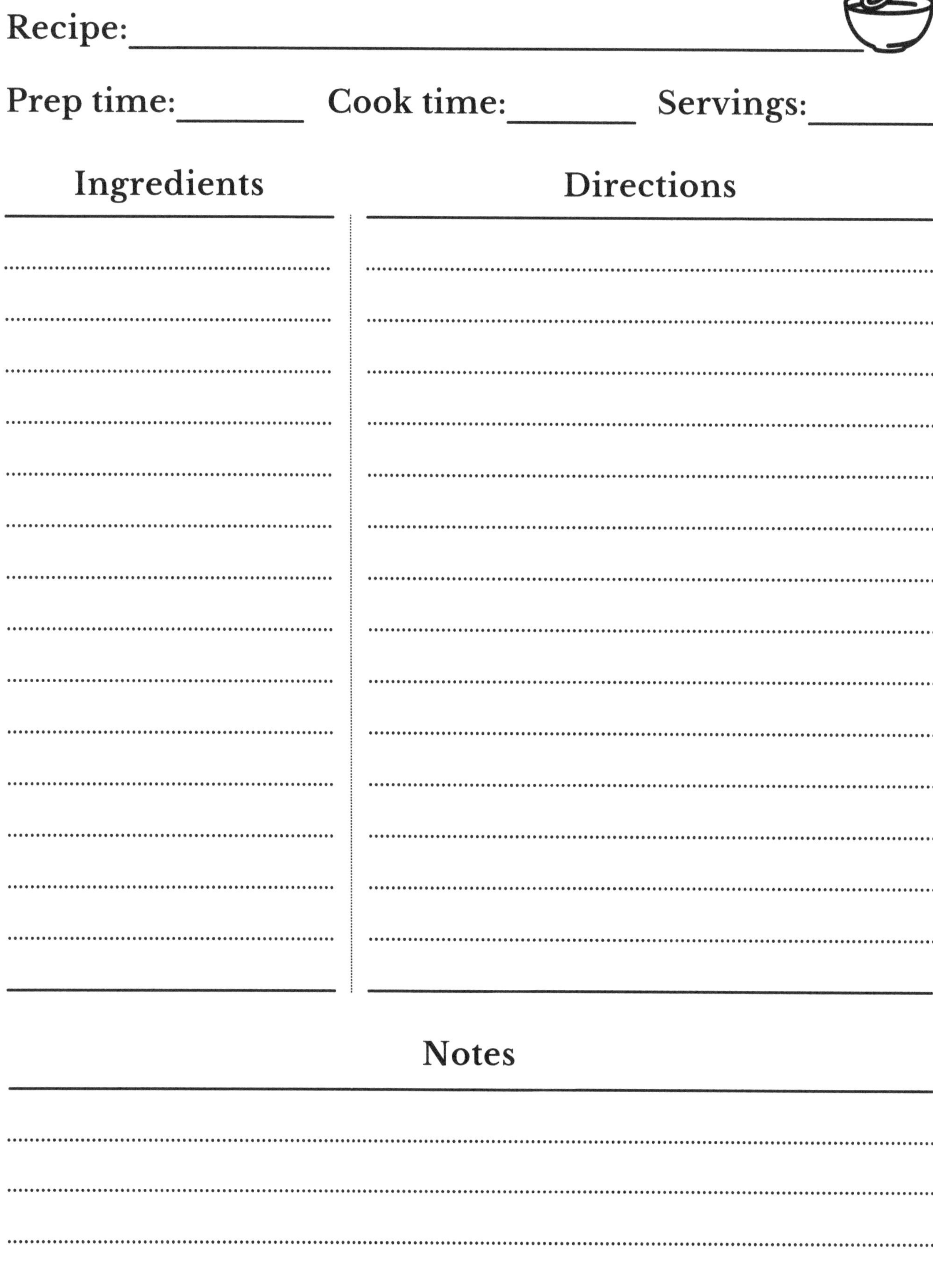

Recipe:_______________________________________

Prep time:________ Cook time:________ Servings:________

Ingredients	Directions

Notes

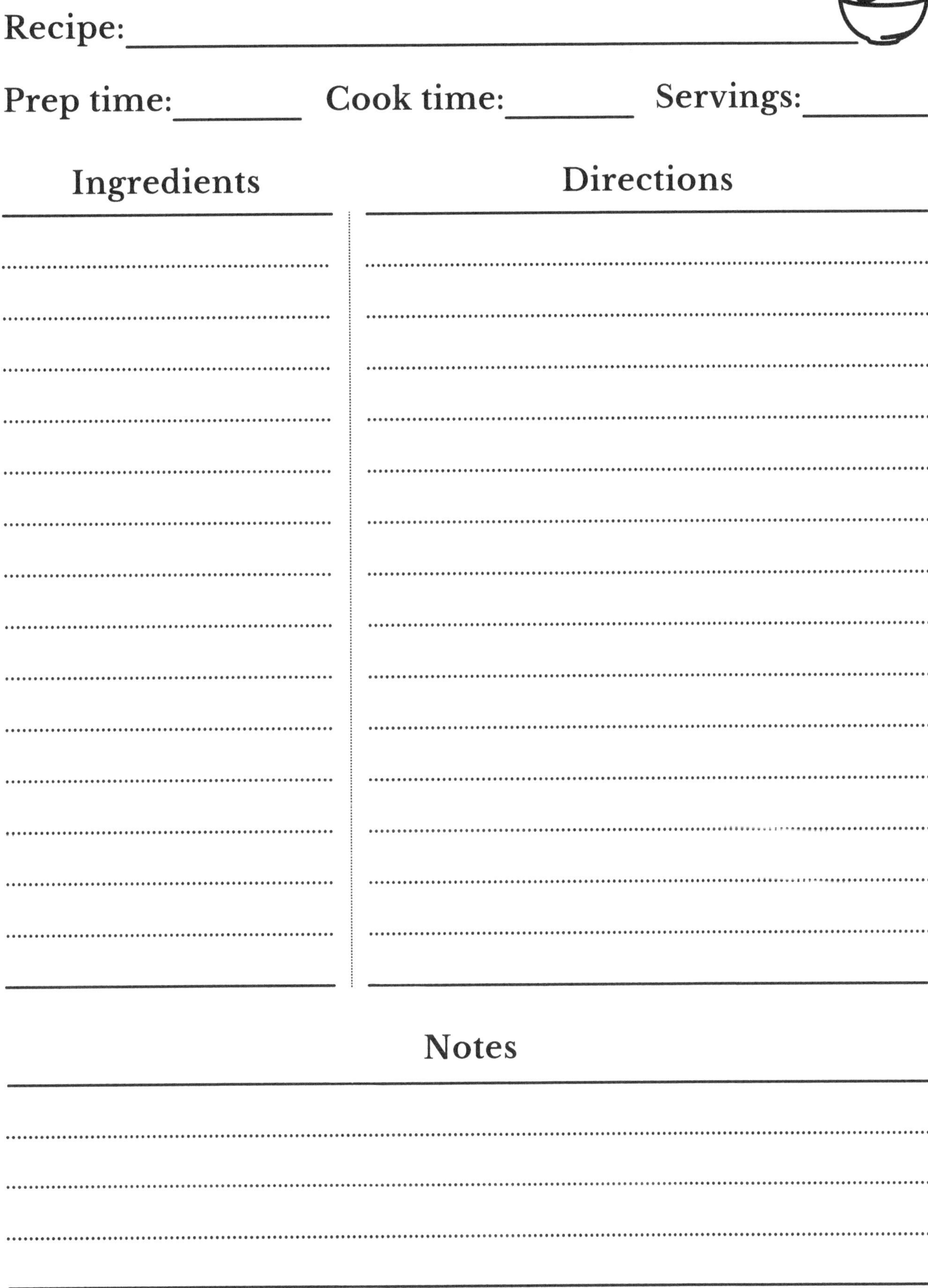

Recipe:

Prep time: _______ **Cook time:** _______ **Servings:** _______

Ingredients

Directions

Notes

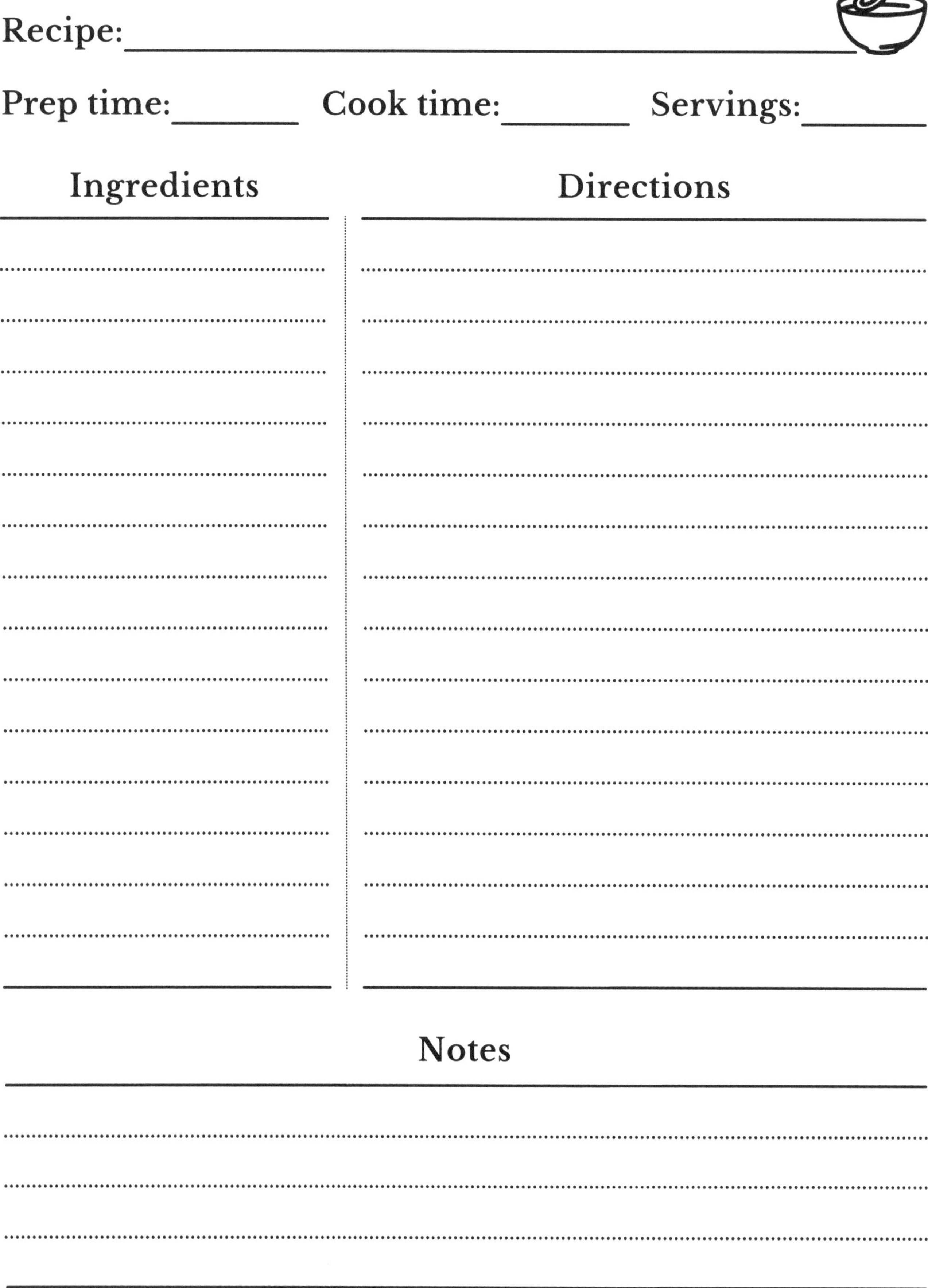

Recipe:____

Prep time:________ **Cook time:**________ **Servings:**________

Ingredients	Directions

Notes

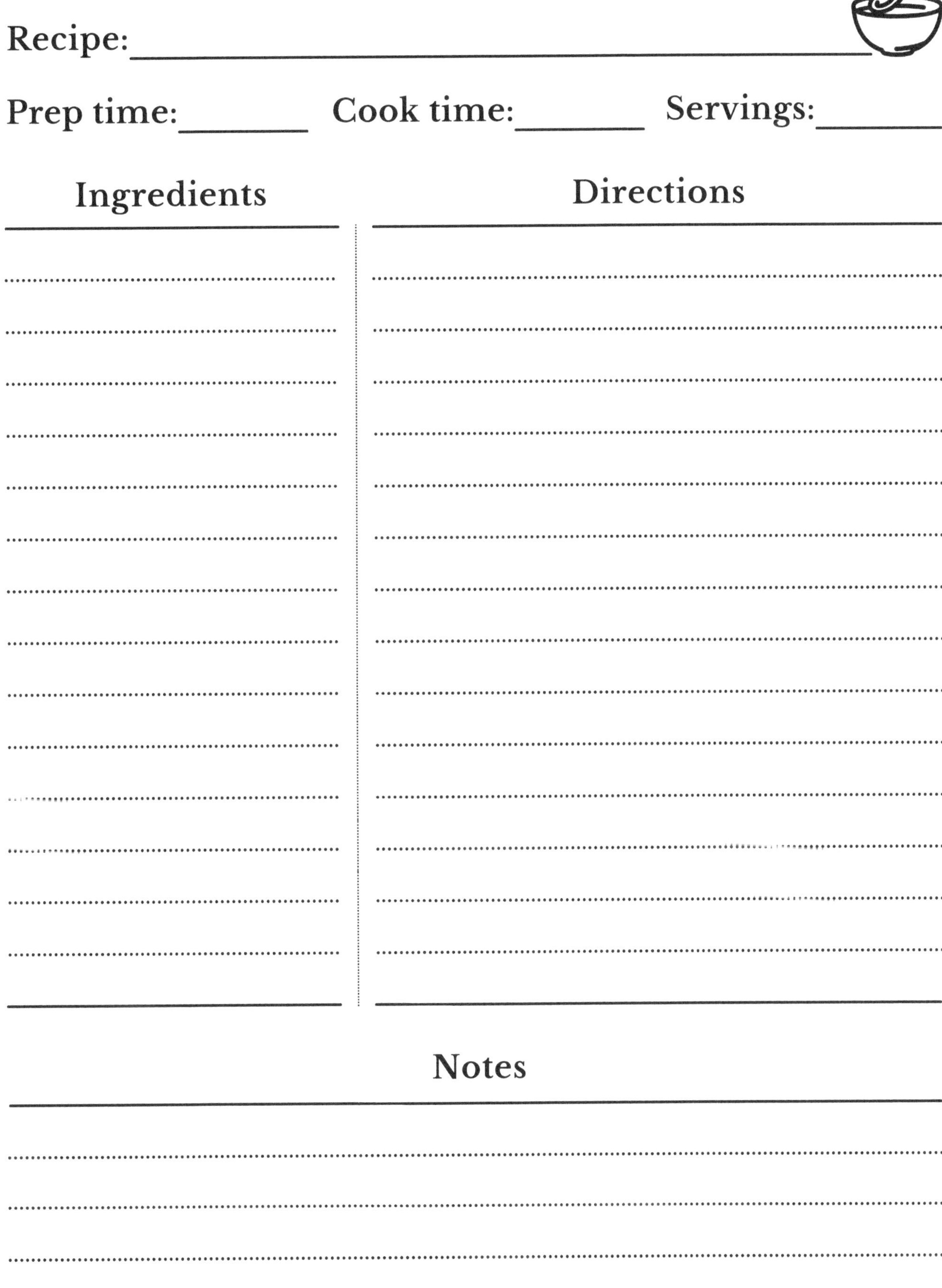

Recipe:____

Prep time:________ Cook time:________ Servings:________

Ingredients

Directions

Notes

Recipe:____

Prep time:_______   Cook time:_______   Servings:_______

Ingredients

Directions

Notes

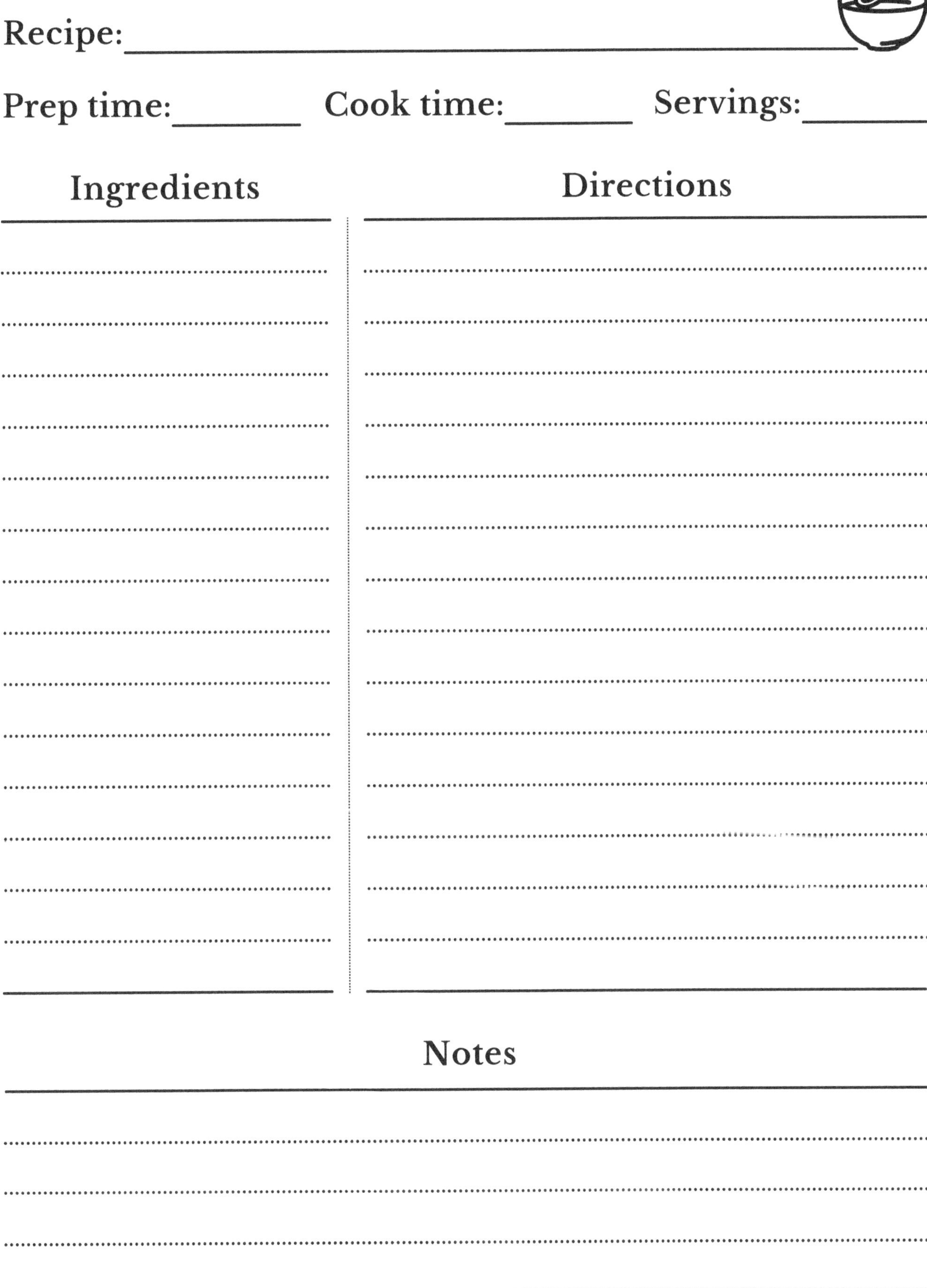

Recipe:_______________________________________

Prep time:________ Cook time:________ Servings:________

Ingredients

Directions

Notes

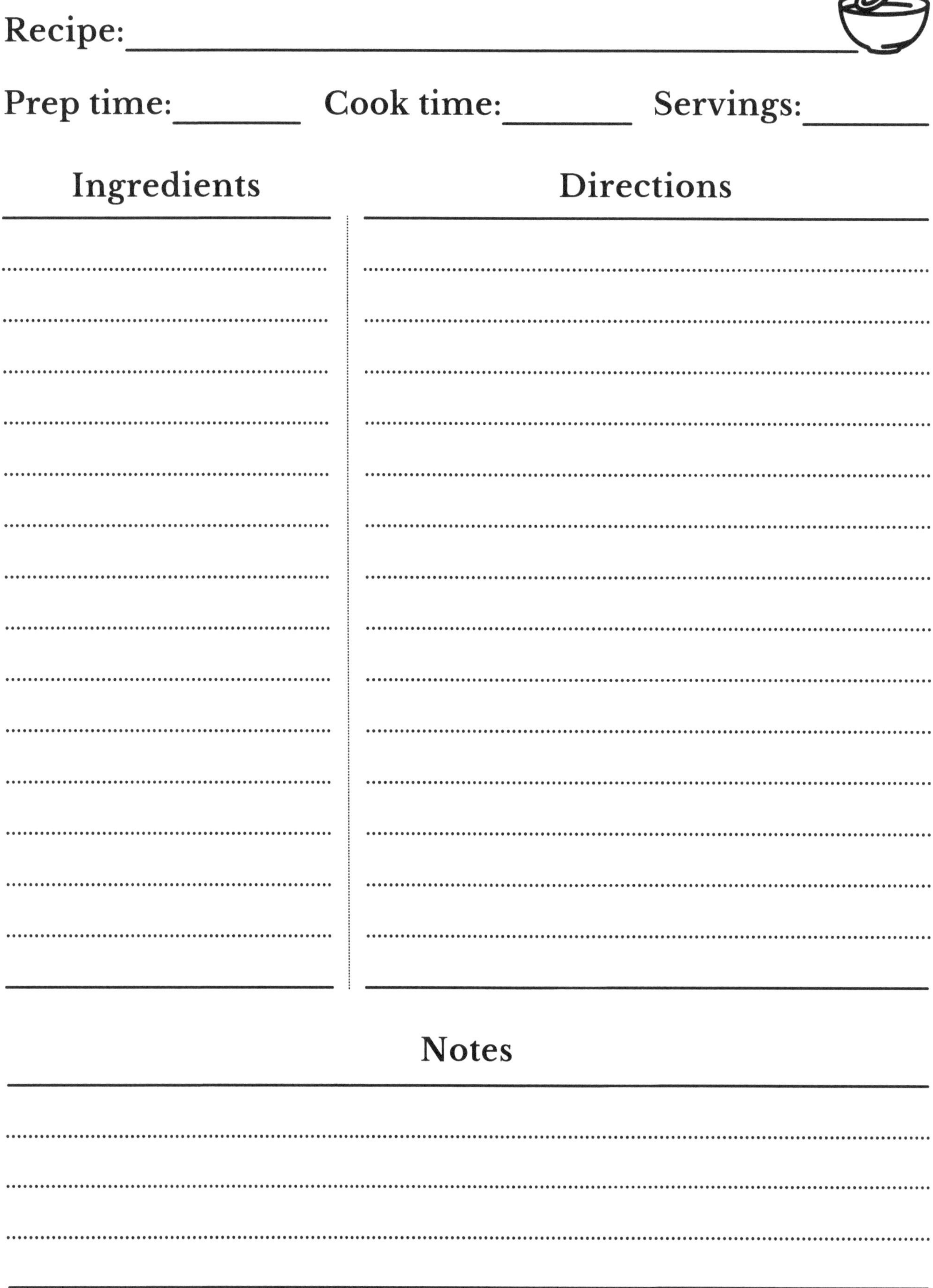

Recipe:____

Prep time:________ Cook time:________ Servings:________

Ingredients

Directions

Notes

Recipe:____ 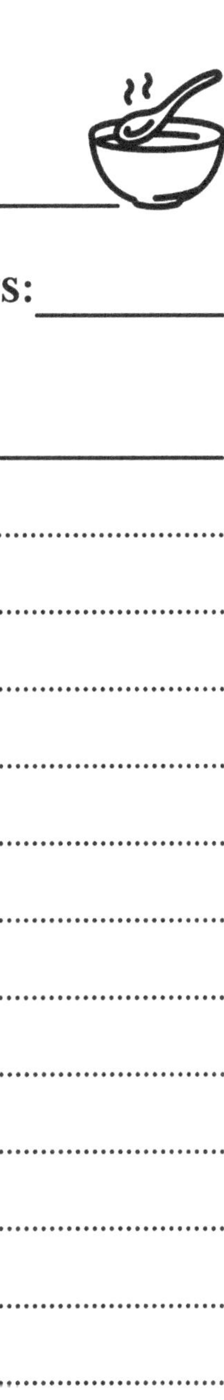

Prep time:_______   Cook time:_______   Servings:_______

Ingredients	Directions

Notes

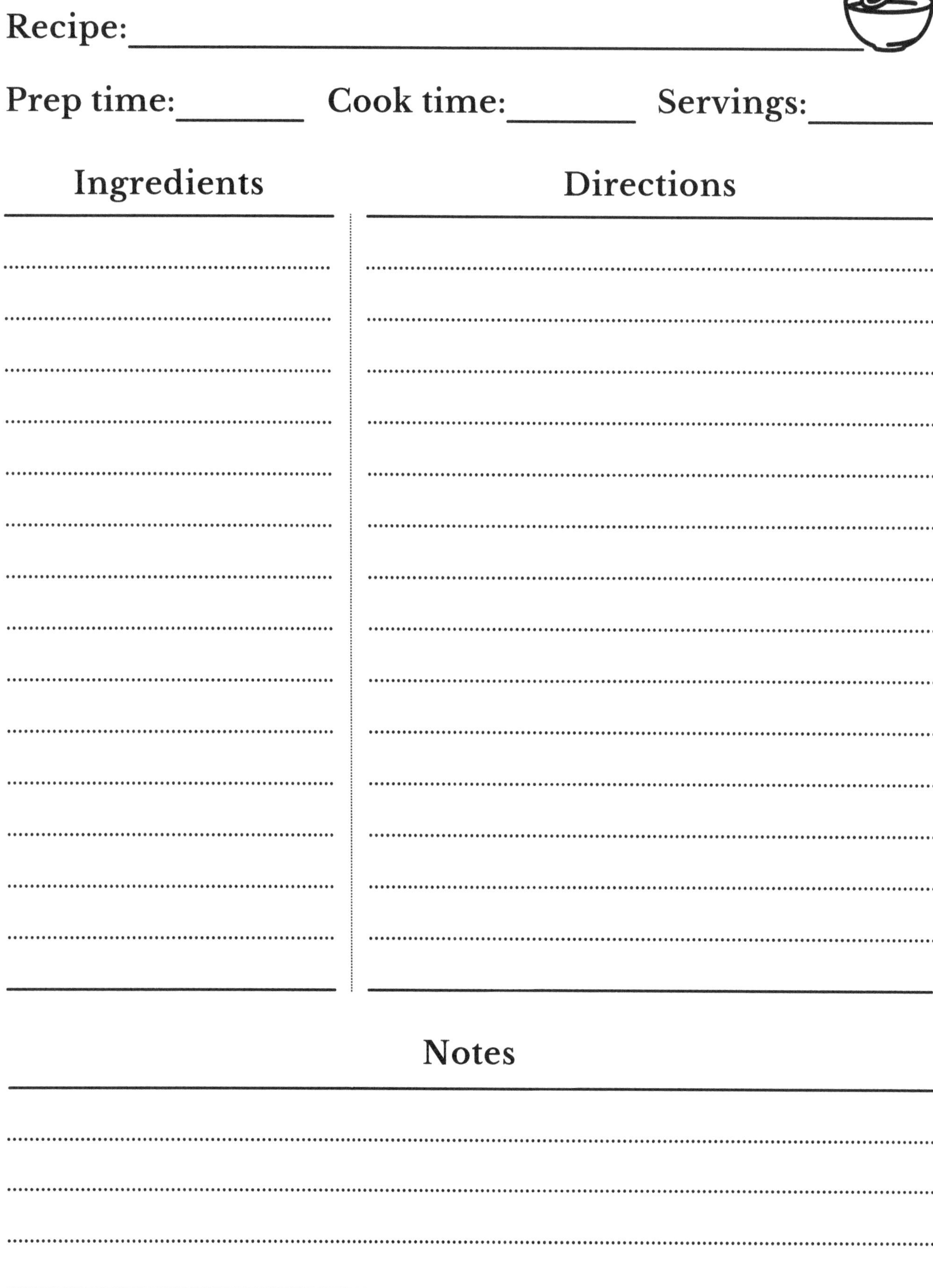

Recipe:____

Prep time:________ Cook time:________ Servings:________

Ingredients

Directions

Notes

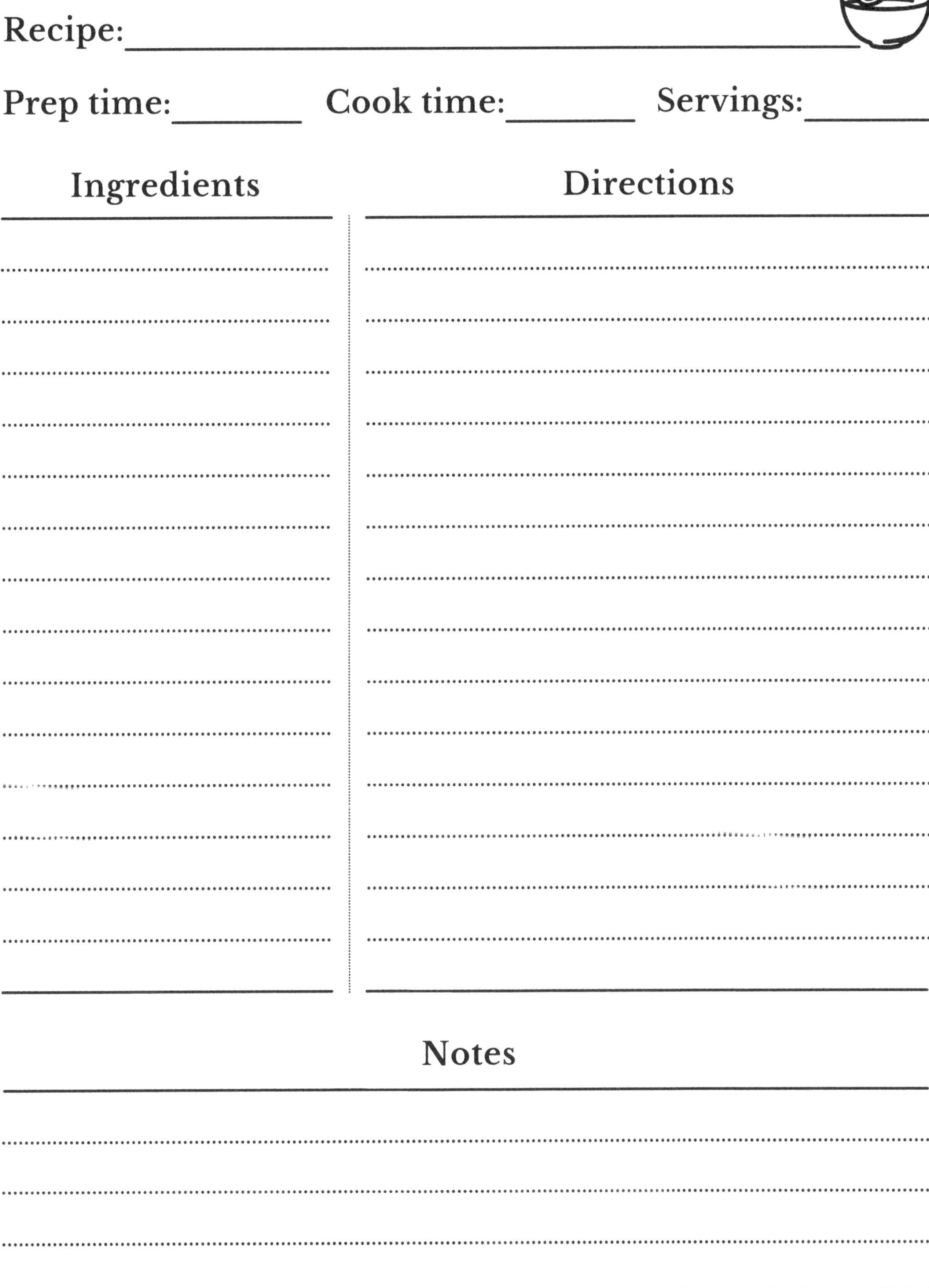

Recipe:____

Prep time:________   Cook time:________   Servings:________

Ingredients

Directions

Notes

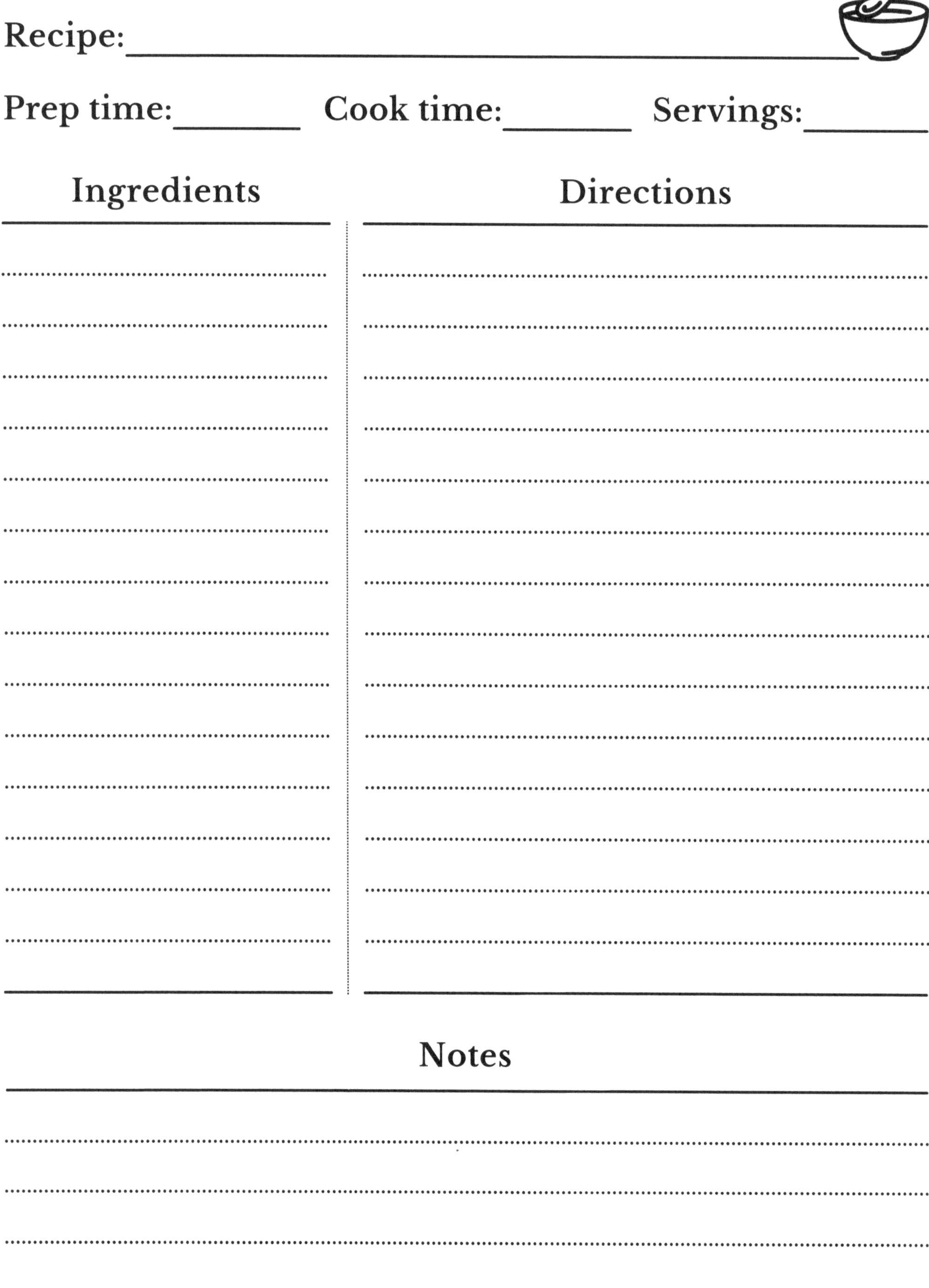

Recipe:____

Prep time:________   Cook time:________   Servings:________

Ingredients

Directions

Notes

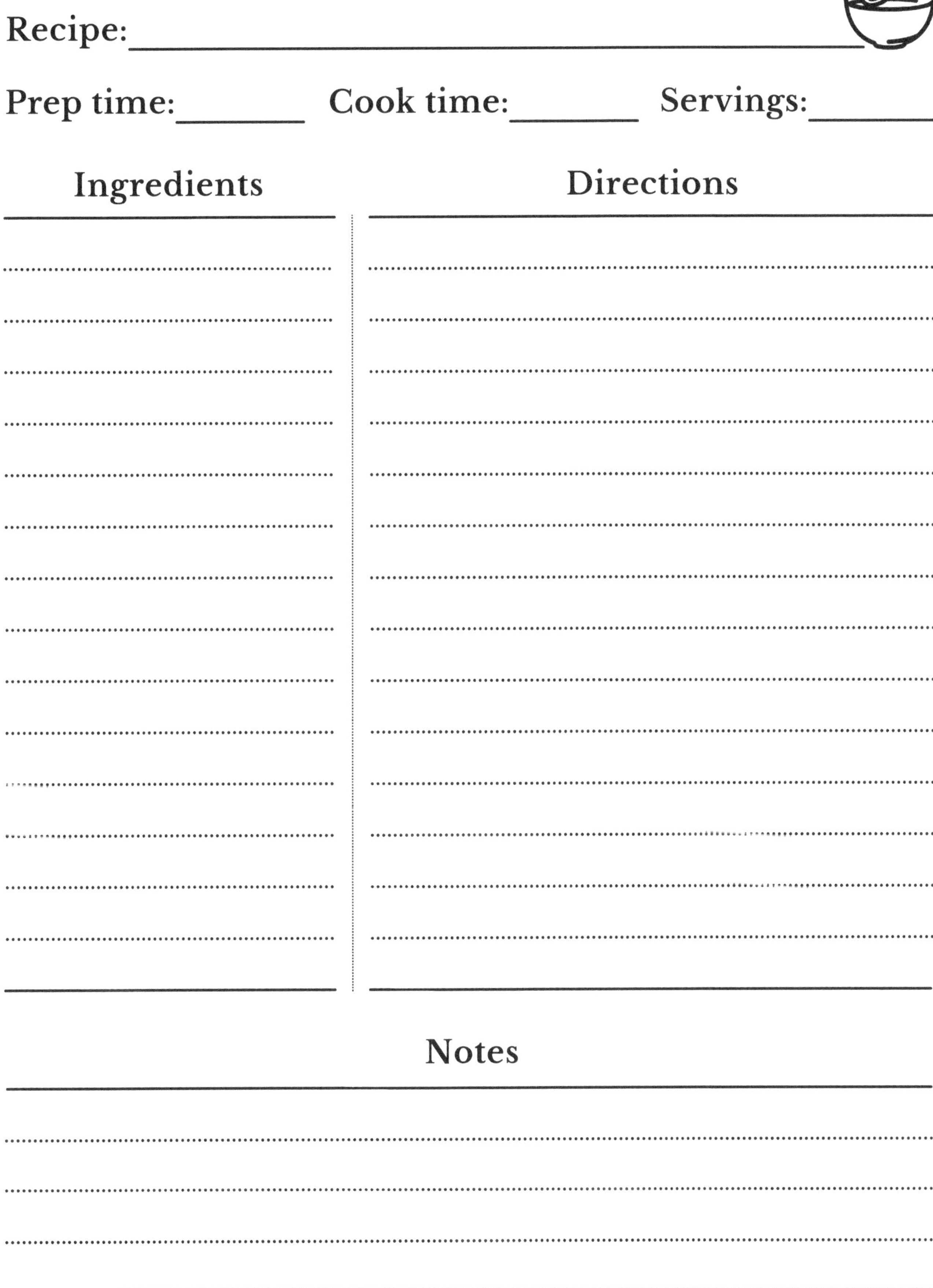

Recipe:____

Prep time:________ Cook time:________ Servings:________

Ingredients

Directions

Notes

Recipe:_________________________ 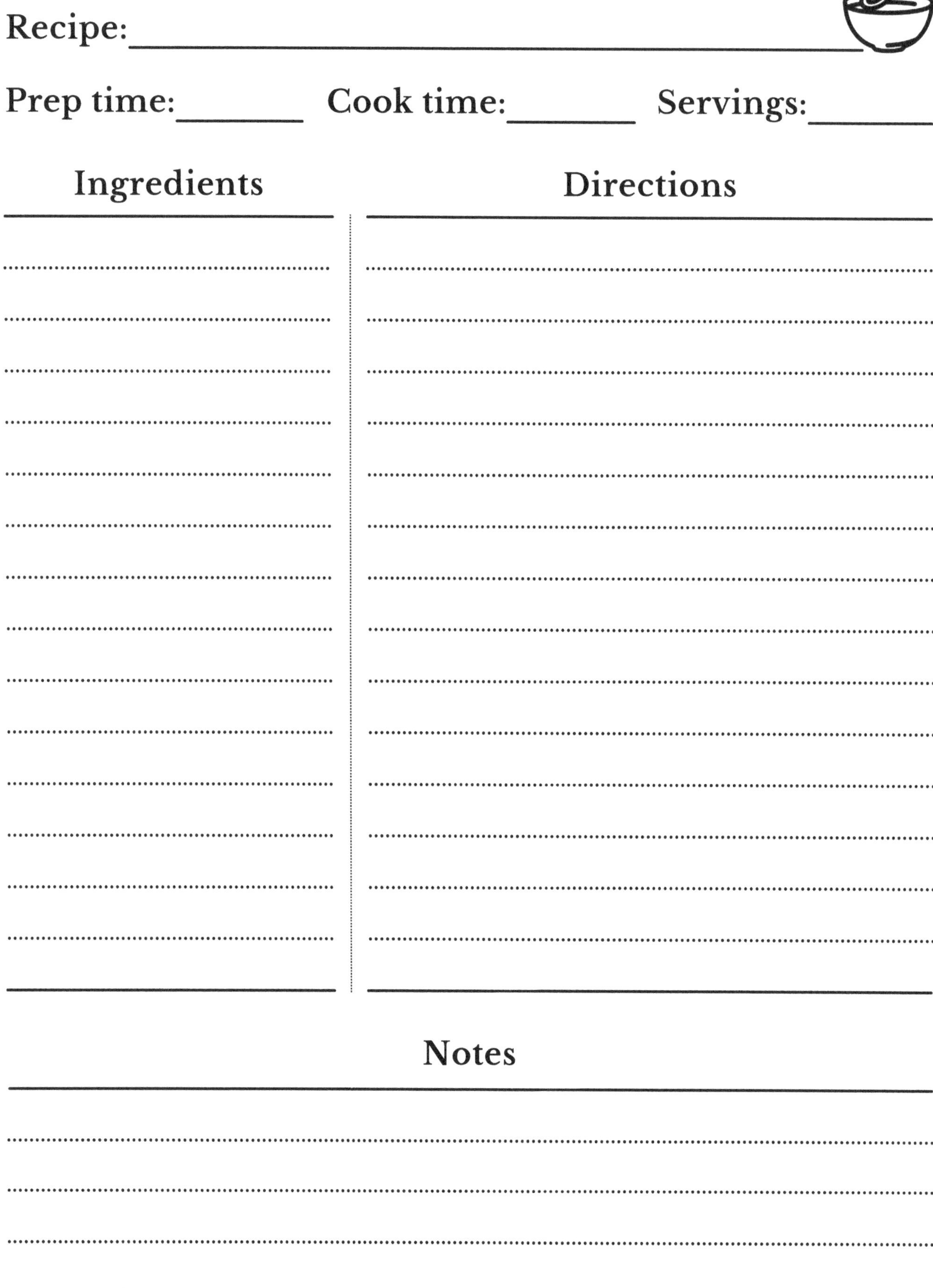

Prep time:______ Cook time:______ Servings:______

Ingredients

Directions

Notes

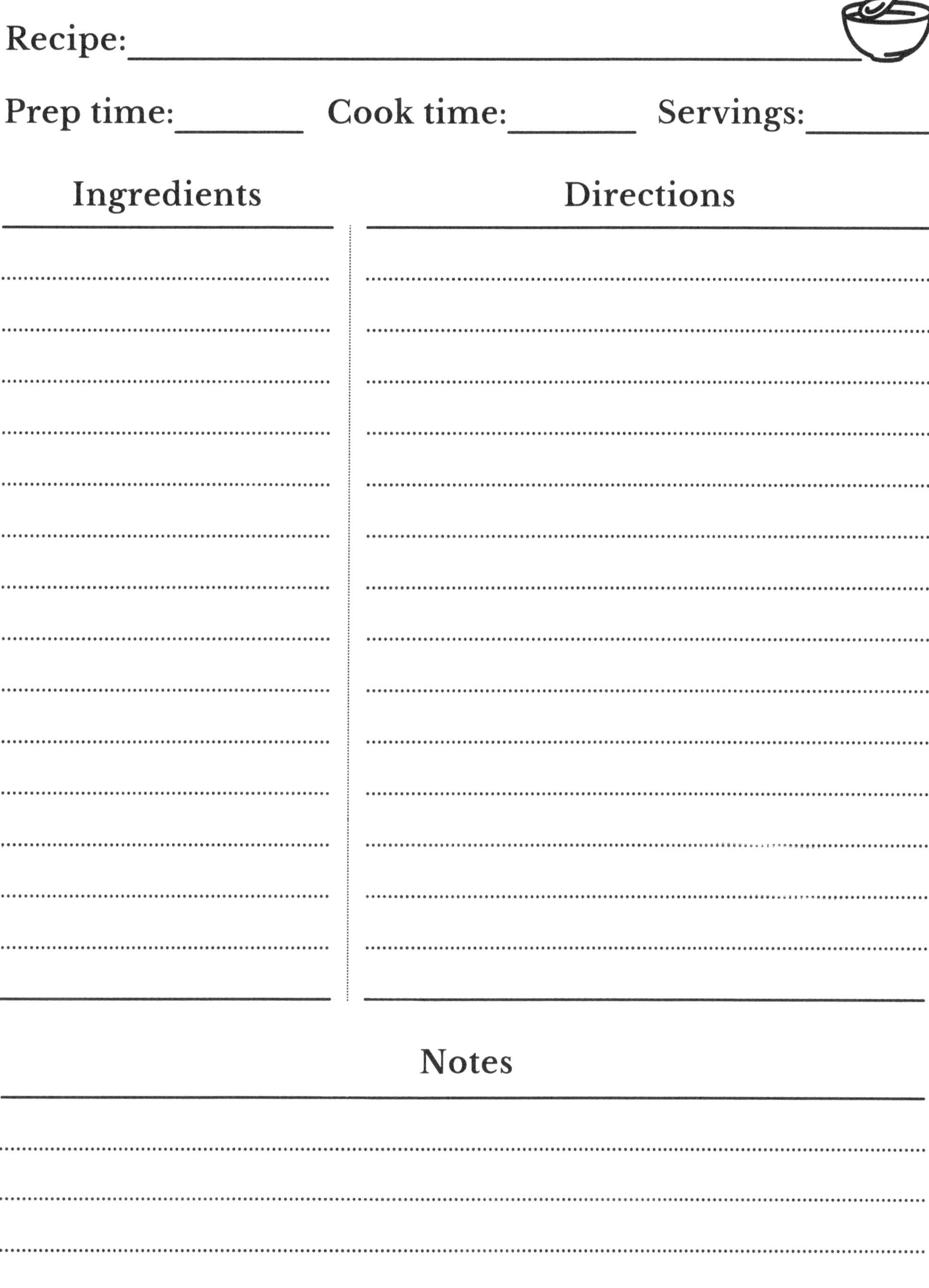

Recipe: _______________________________

Prep time: _______ Cook time: _______ Servings: _______

Ingredients

Directions

Notes

Recipe:____

Prep time:_______   Cook time:_______   Servings:_______

Ingredients   ## Directions

Notes

Recipe: _______________________________

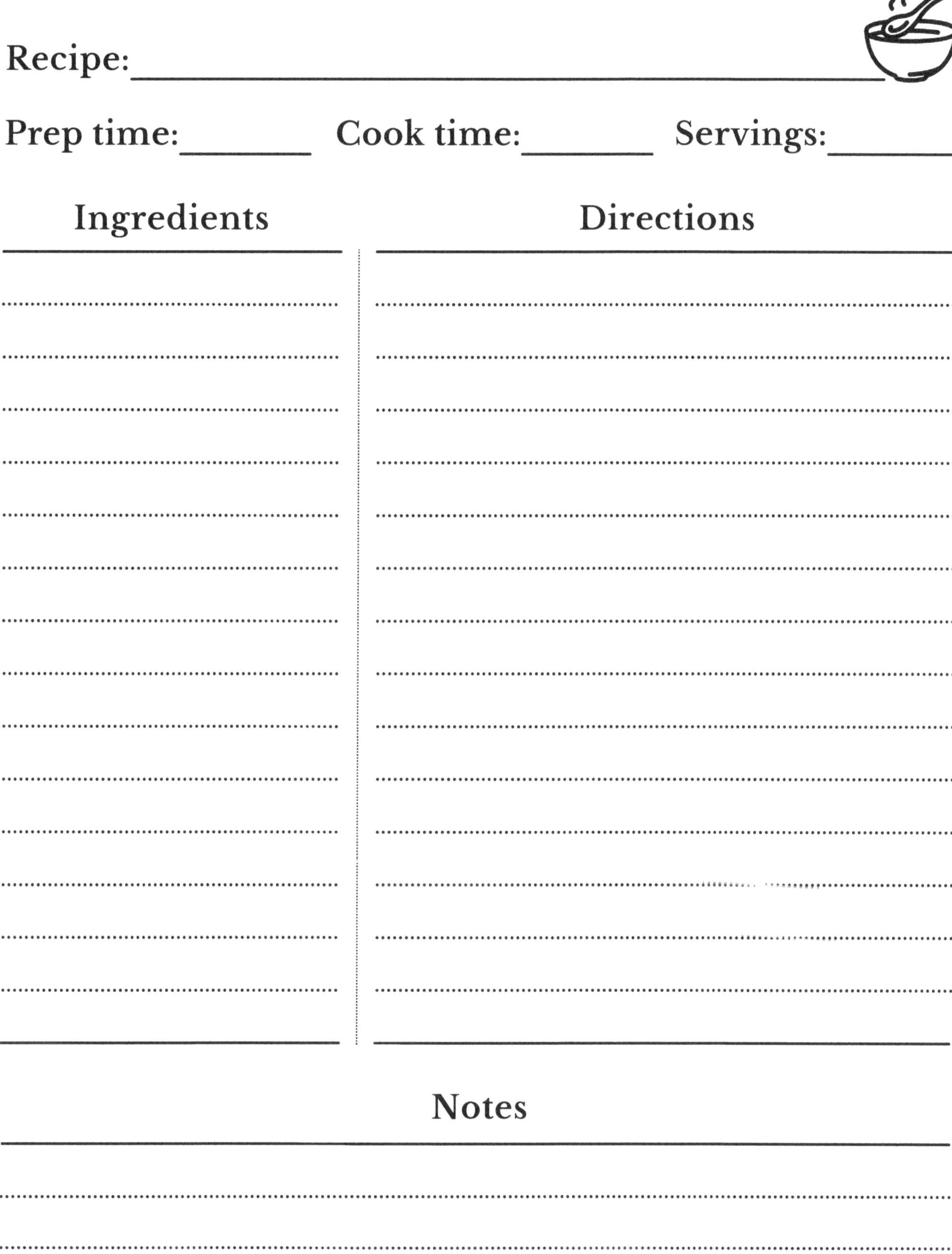

Prep time: _______ Cook time: _______ Servings: _______

Ingredients   Directions

Notes

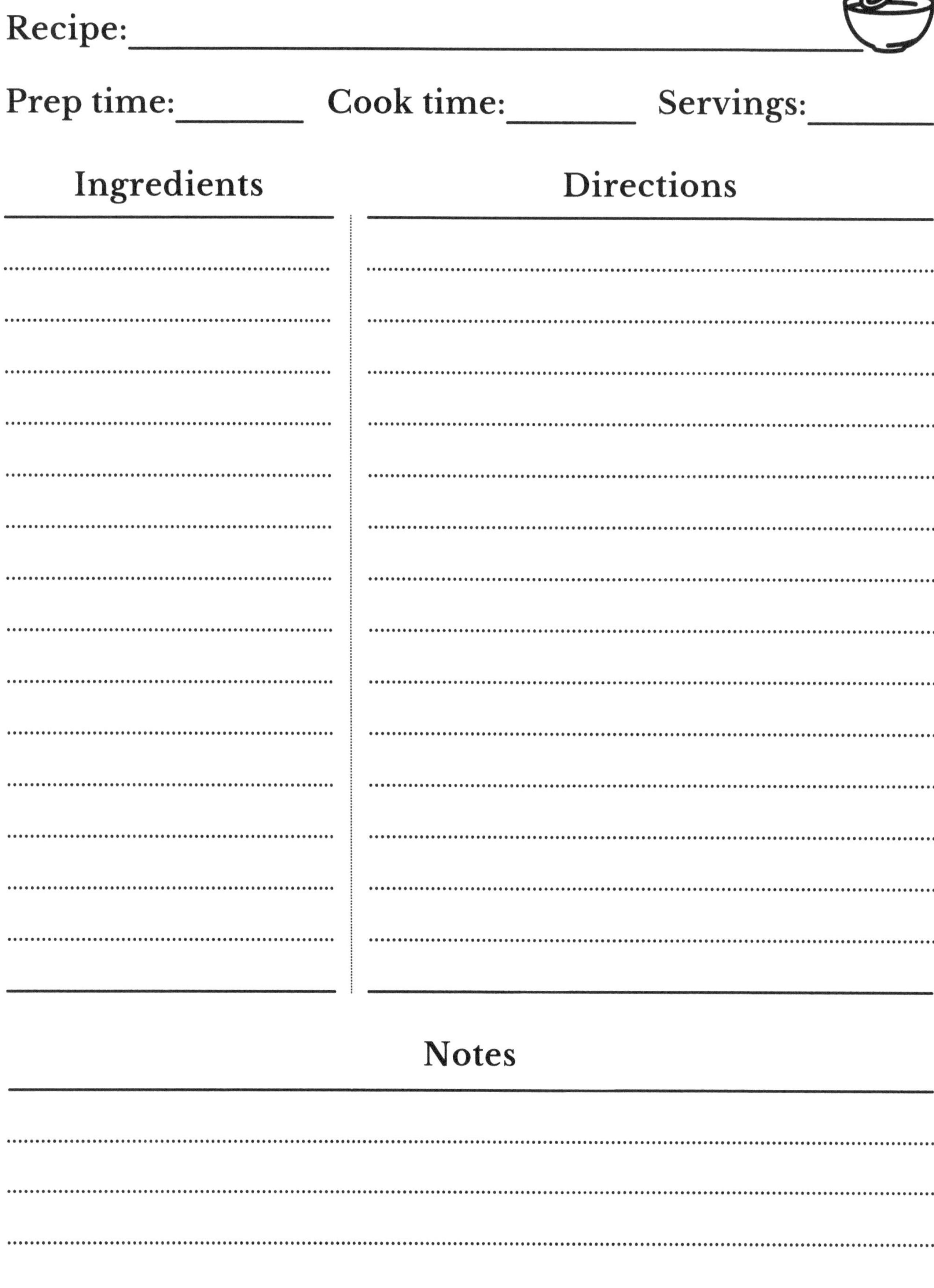

Recipe:_______________________________________

Prep time:______   Cook time:______   Servings:______

Ingredients

Directions

Notes

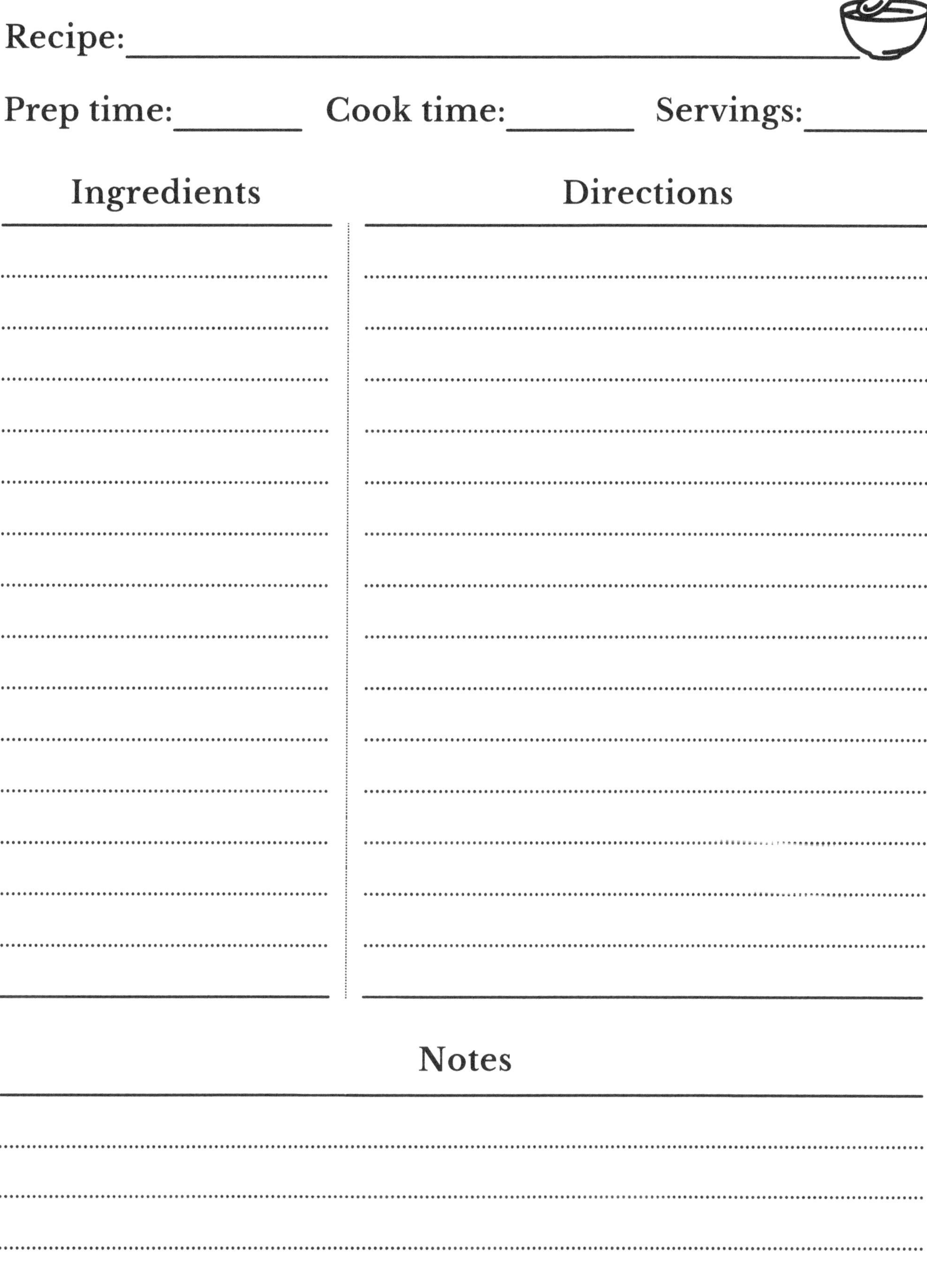

Recipe:____

Prep time:_________ Cook time:_________ Servings:_________

Ingredients	Directions

Notes

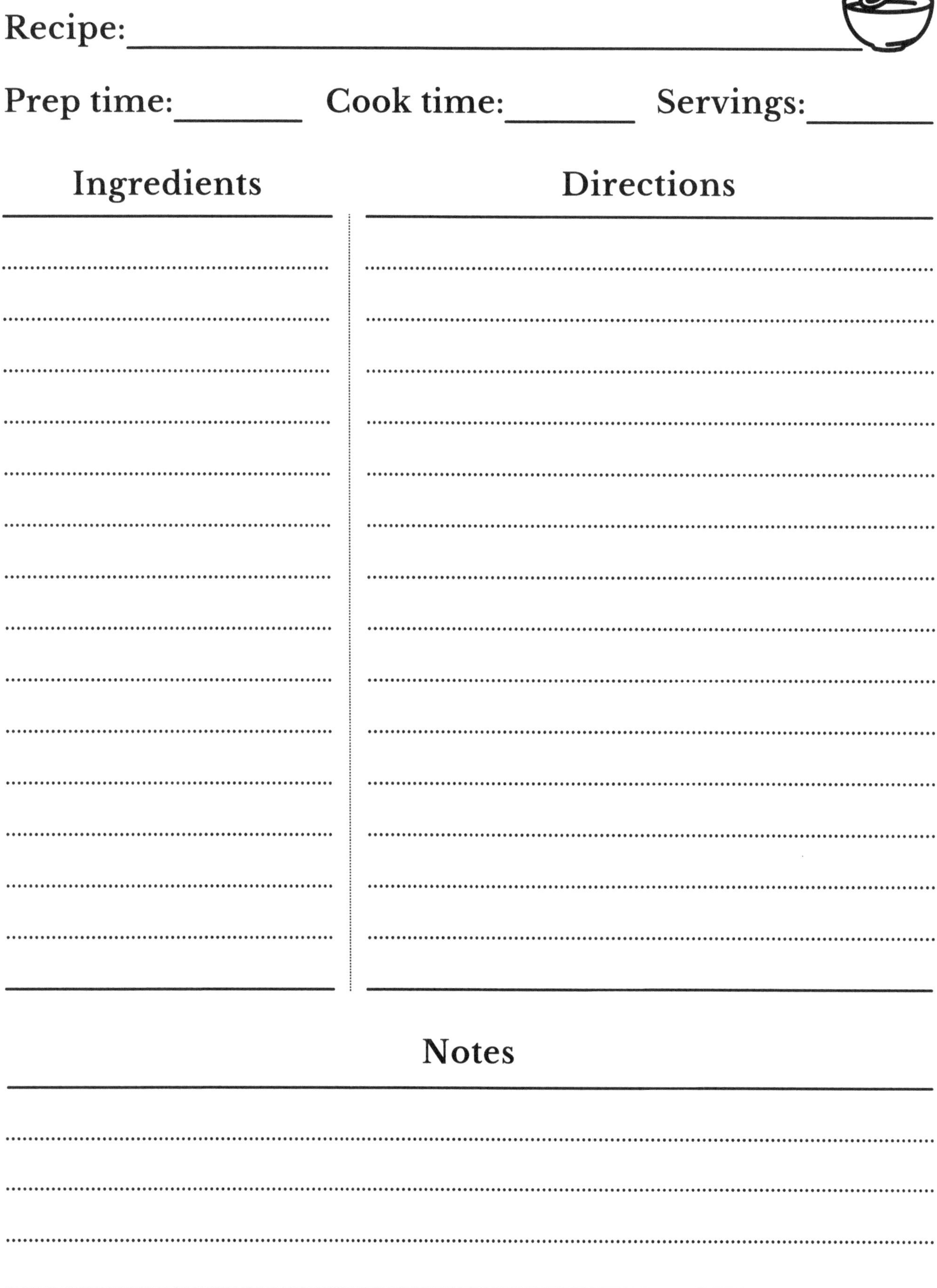

Recipe:____

Prep time:________ Cook time:________ Servings:________

Ingredients	Directions

Notes

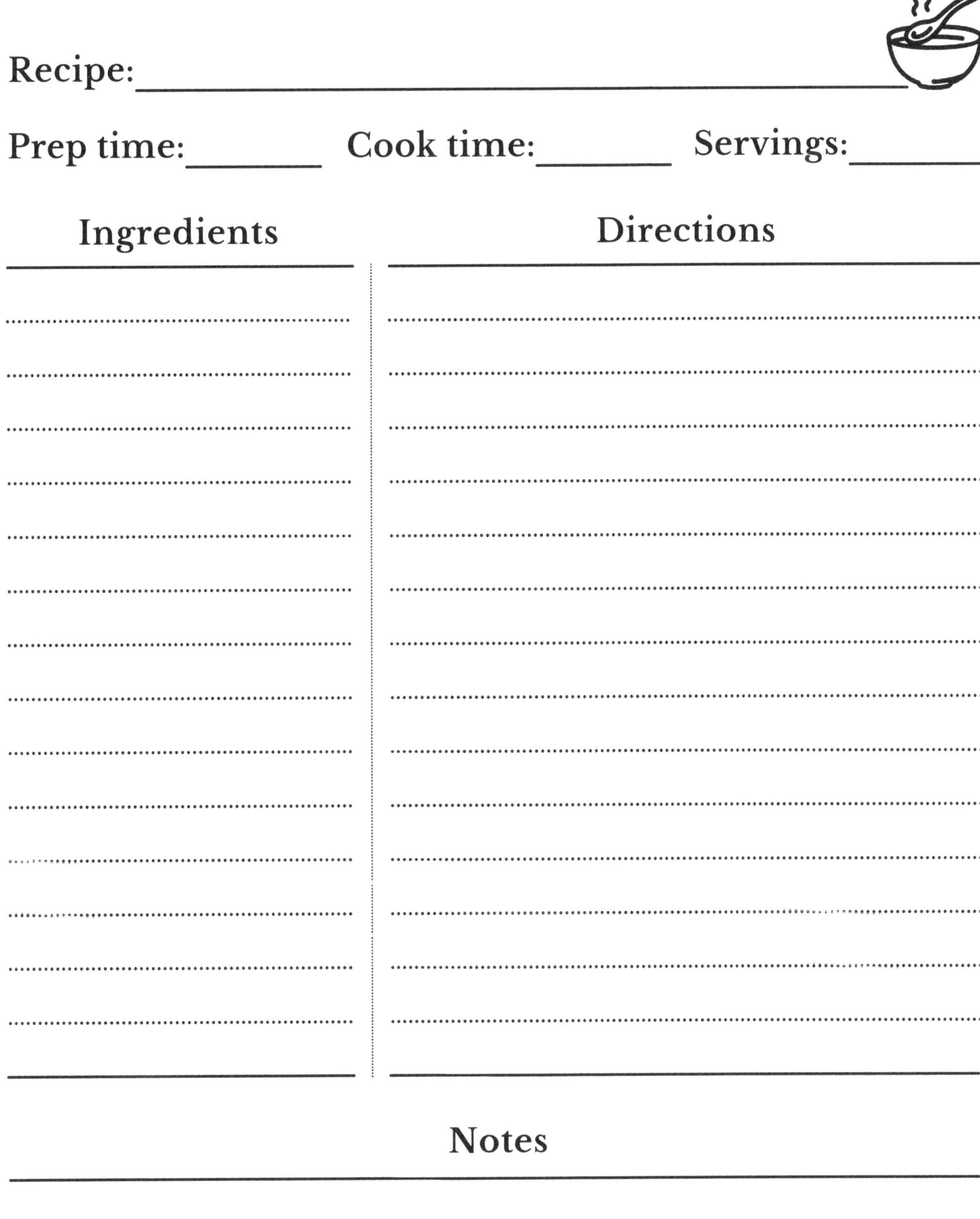

Recipe:____

Prep time:_______   Cook time:_______   Servings:_______

Ingredients

Directions

Notes

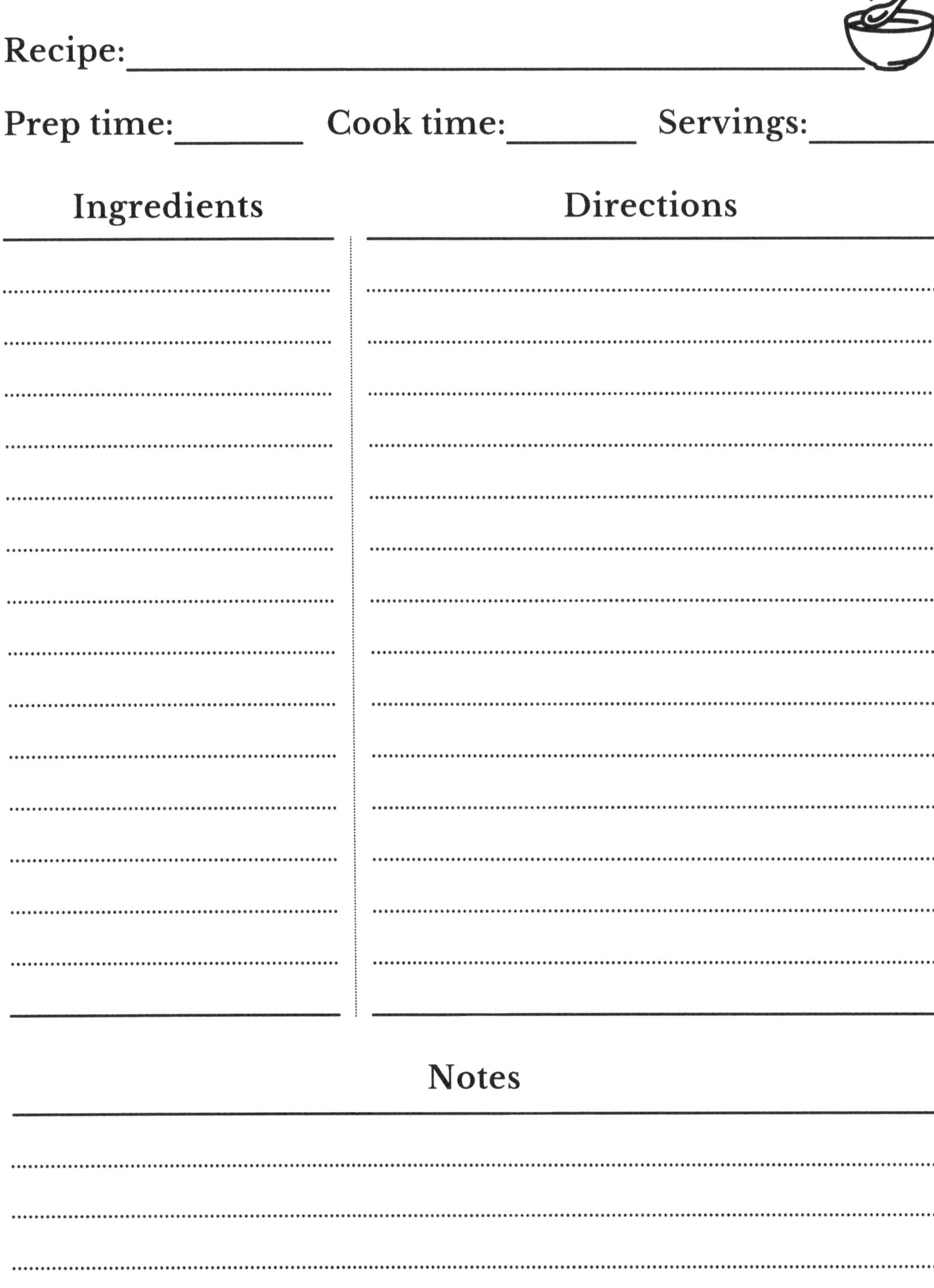

Recipe:____

Prep time:________ Cook time:________ Servings:________

Ingredients

Directions

Notes

Recipe:____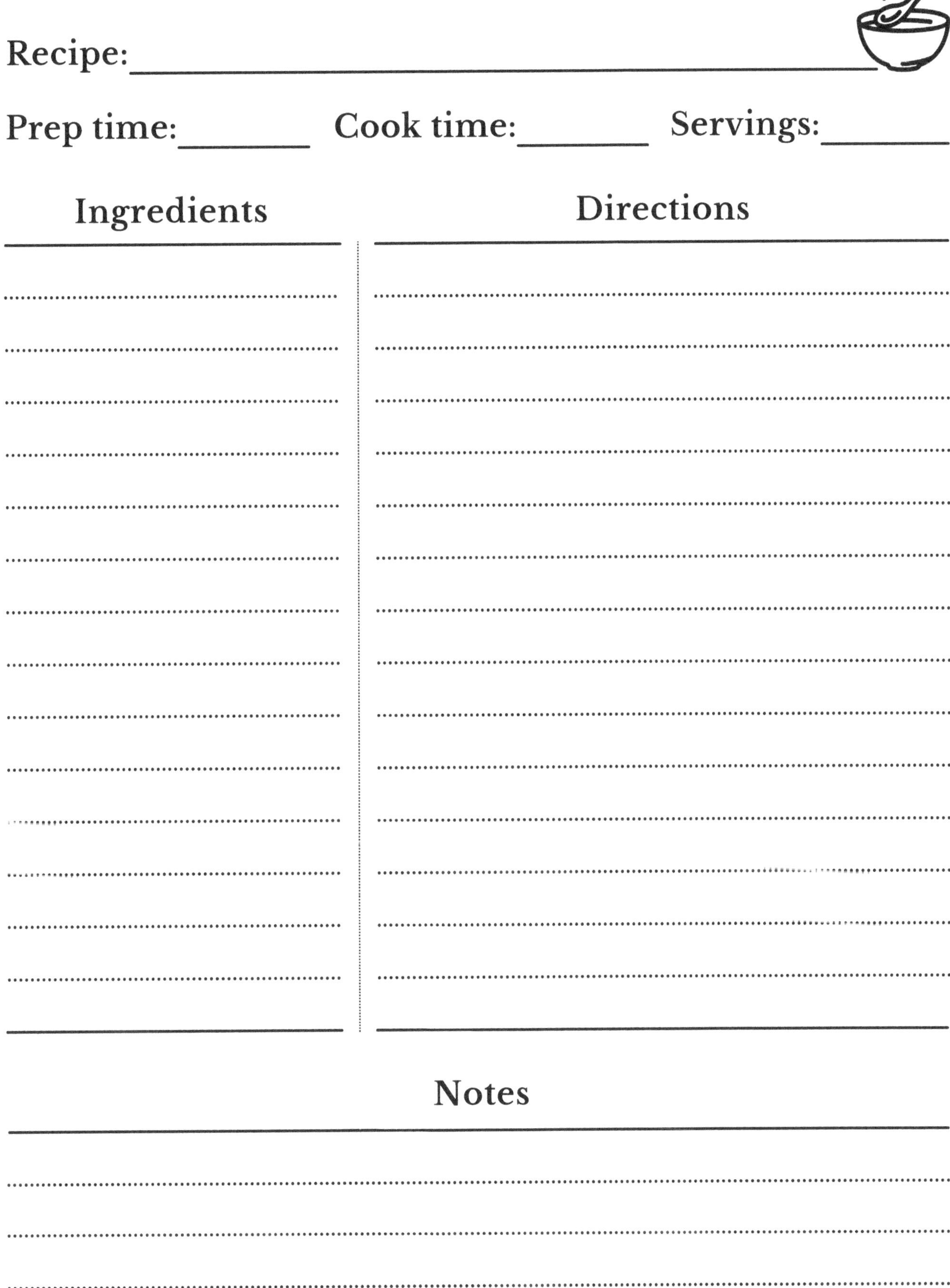

Prep time:_______   Cook time:_______   Servings:_______

Ingredients

Directions

Notes

Recipe:_______________________________________ 

Prep time:_______   Cook time:_______   Servings:_______

Ingredients

Directions

Notes

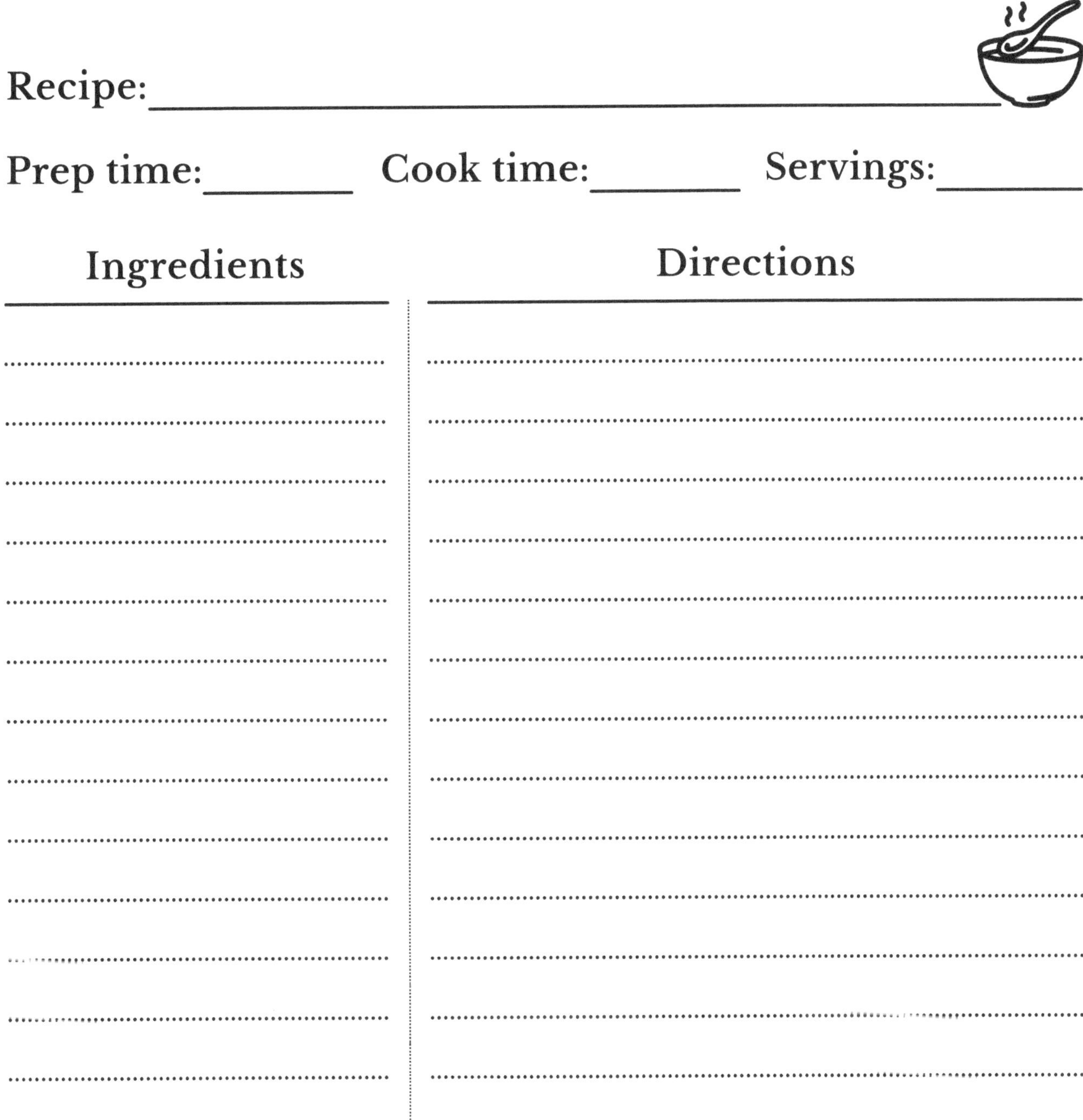

Recipe:____

Prep time:_______ Cook time:_______ Servings:_______

Ingredients

Directions

Notes

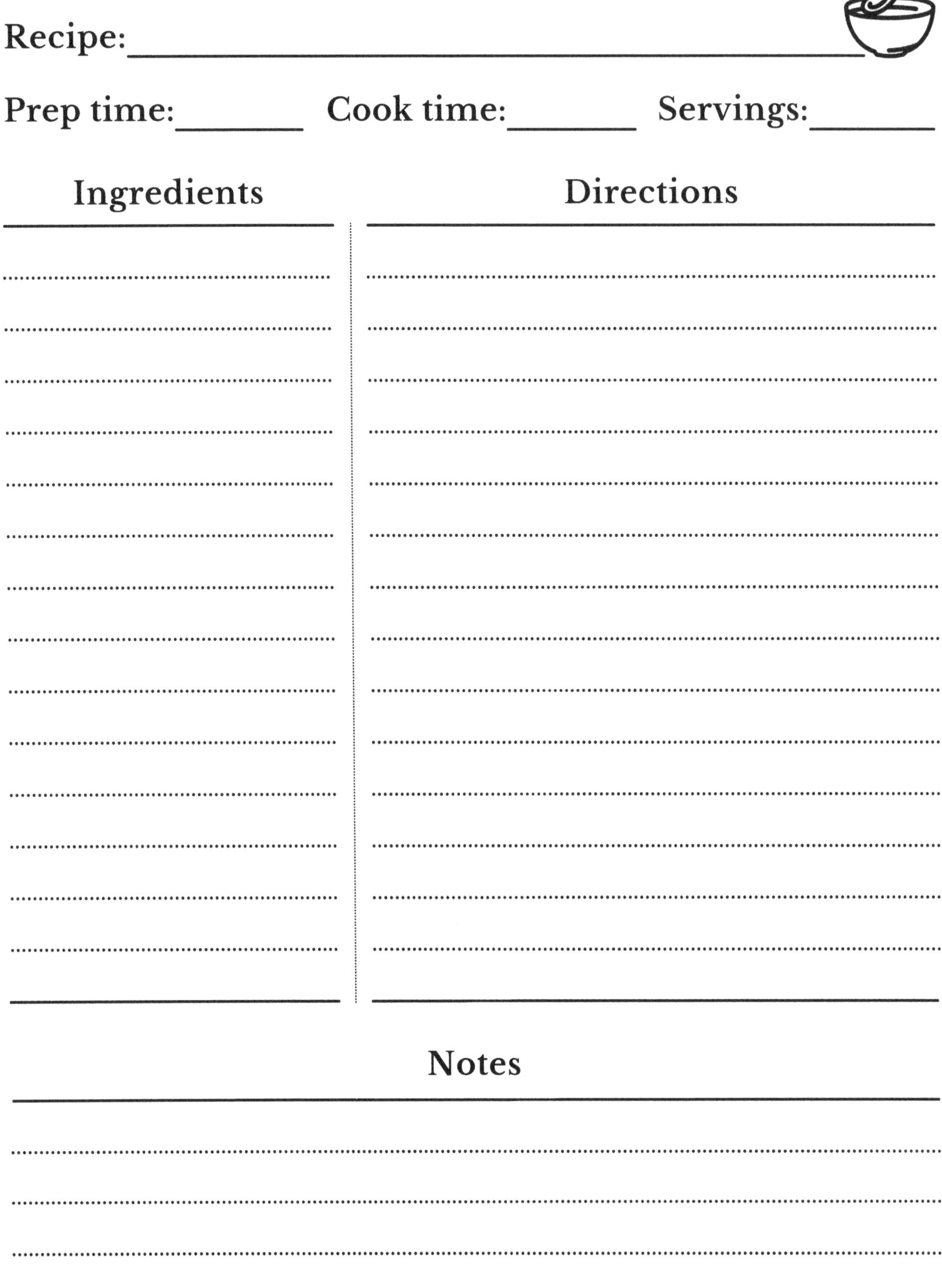

Recipe:____

Prep time:________ Cook time:________ Servings:________

Ingredients

Directions

Notes

Recipe:____ 

Prep time:_______   Cook time:_______   Servings:_______

Ingredients	Directions

Notes

Recipe:

Prep time: _______ **Cook time:** _______ **Servings:** _______

Ingredients

Directions

Notes

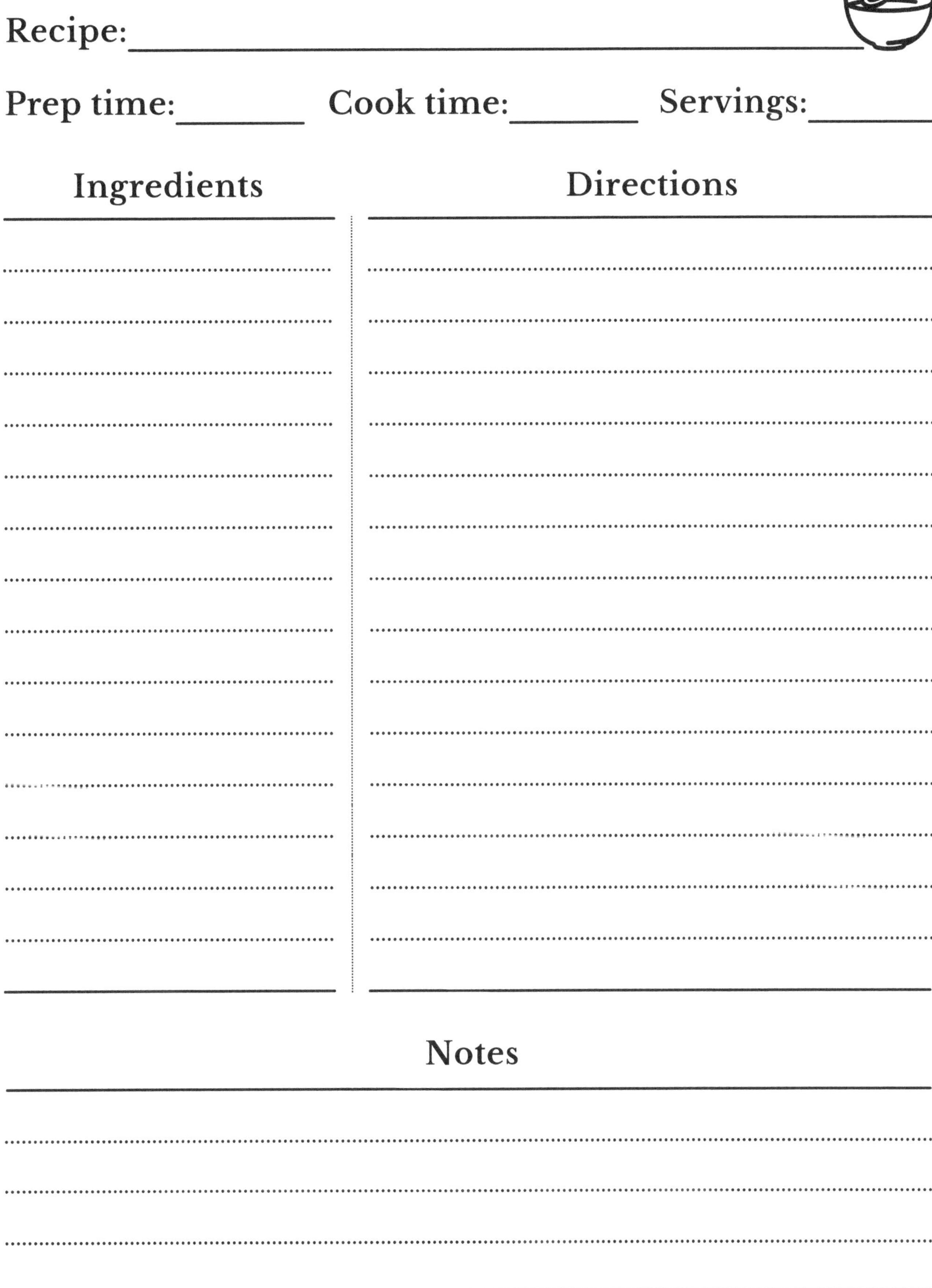

Recipe:____

Prep time:________ Cook time:________ Servings:________

Ingredients

Directions

Notes

Recipe:____ 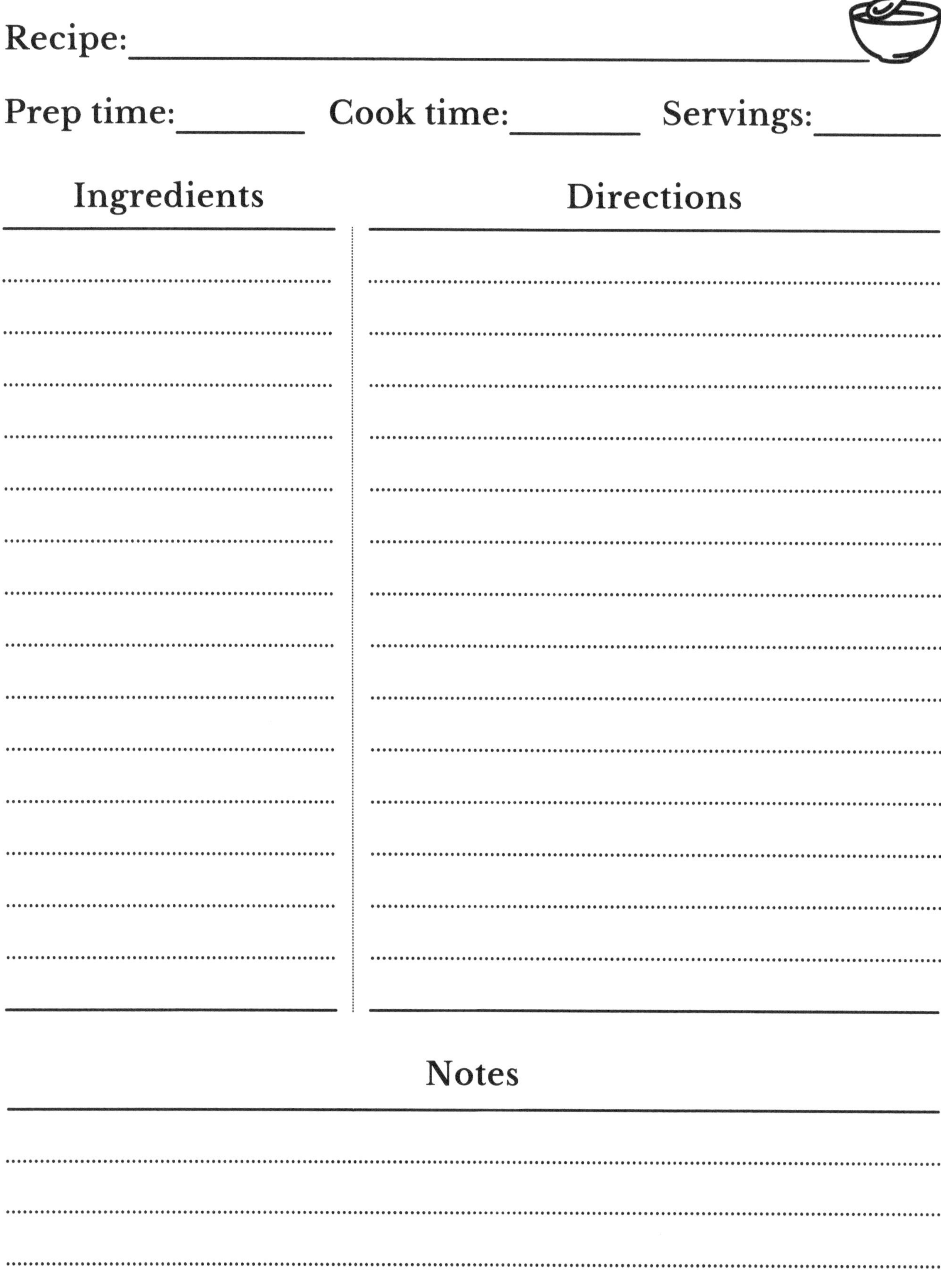

Prep time:_______ Cook time:_______ Servings:_______

Ingredients	Directions

Notes

Recipe:_______________________________________

Prep time:______ **Cook time:**______ **Servings:**______

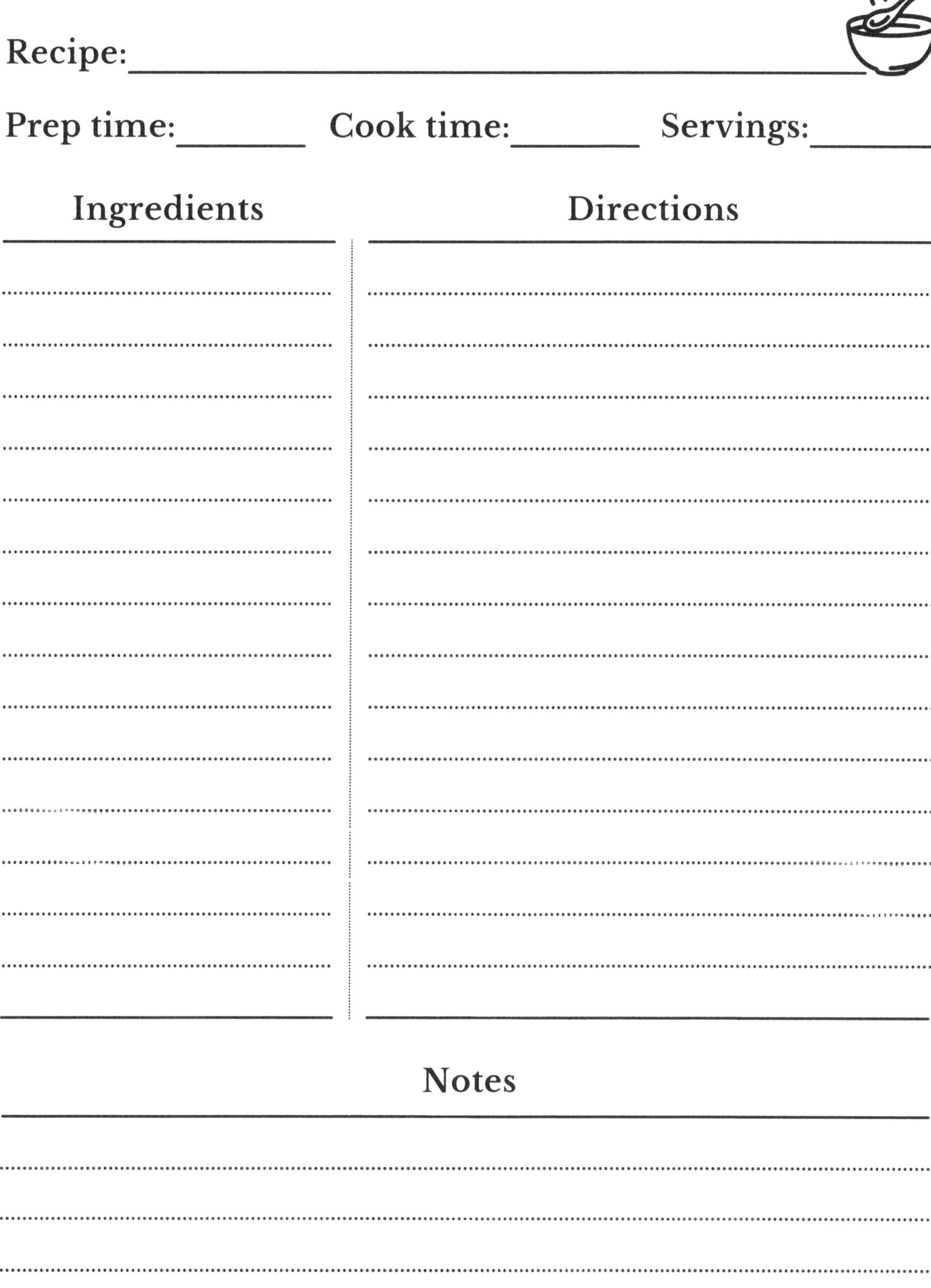

Ingredients

Directions

Notes

Recipe:_______________________________

Prep time:______ Cook time:______ Servings:______

Ingredients

Directions

Notes

Recipe:____ 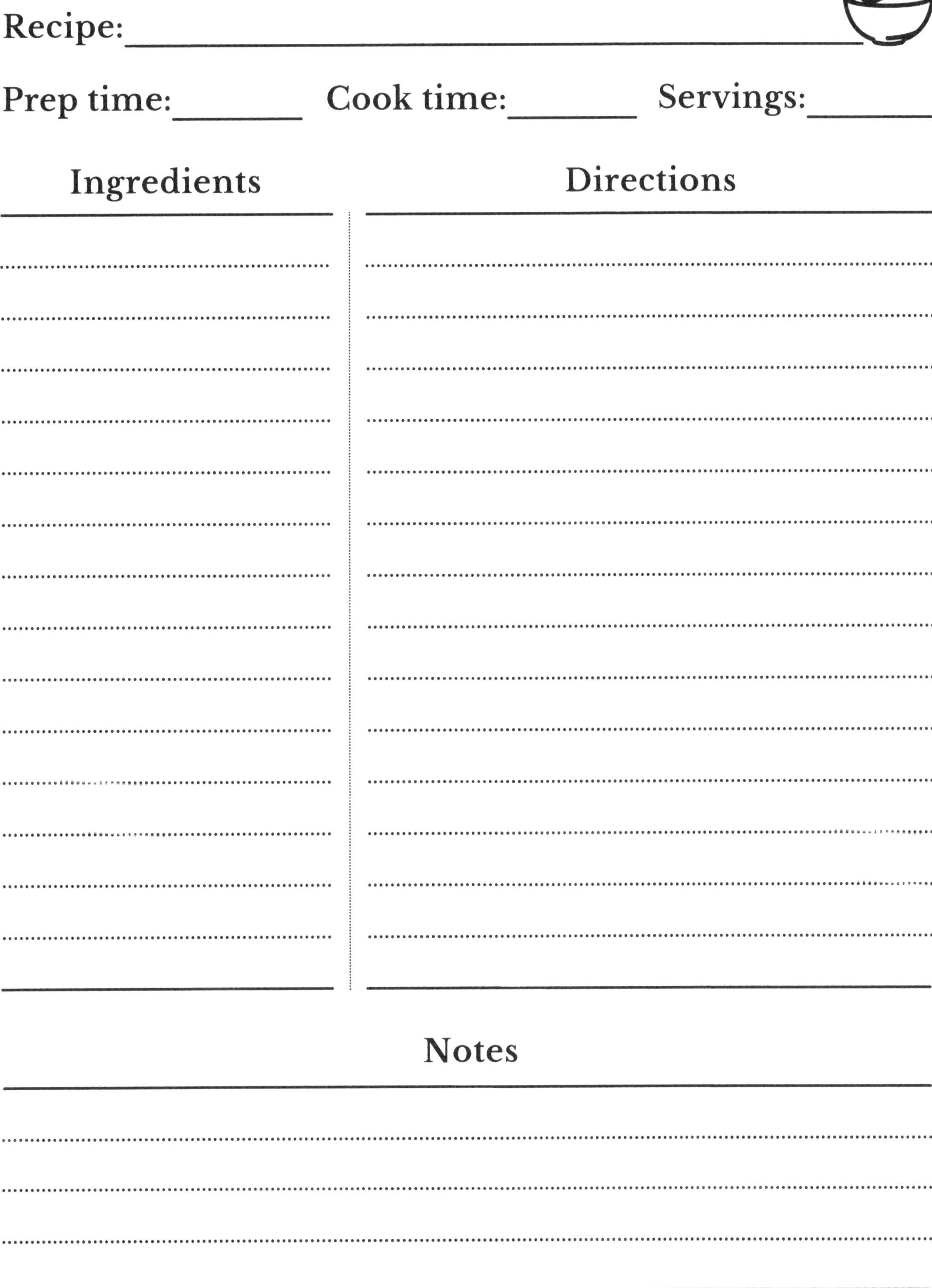

Prep time:_______   Cook time:_______   Servings:_______

Ingredients

Directions

Notes

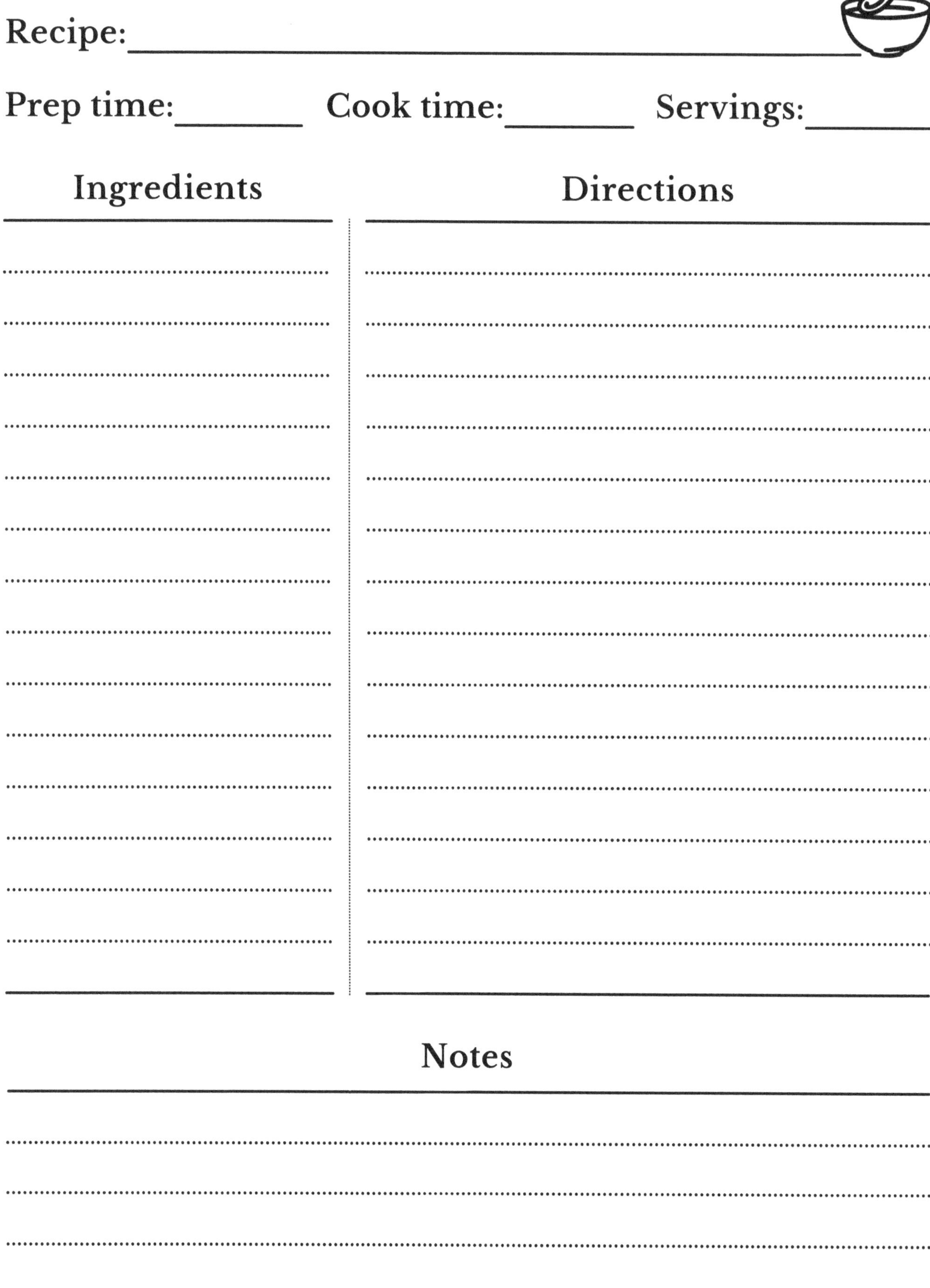

Recipe:

Prep time:_______   Cook time:_______   Servings:_______

Ingredients

Directions

Notes

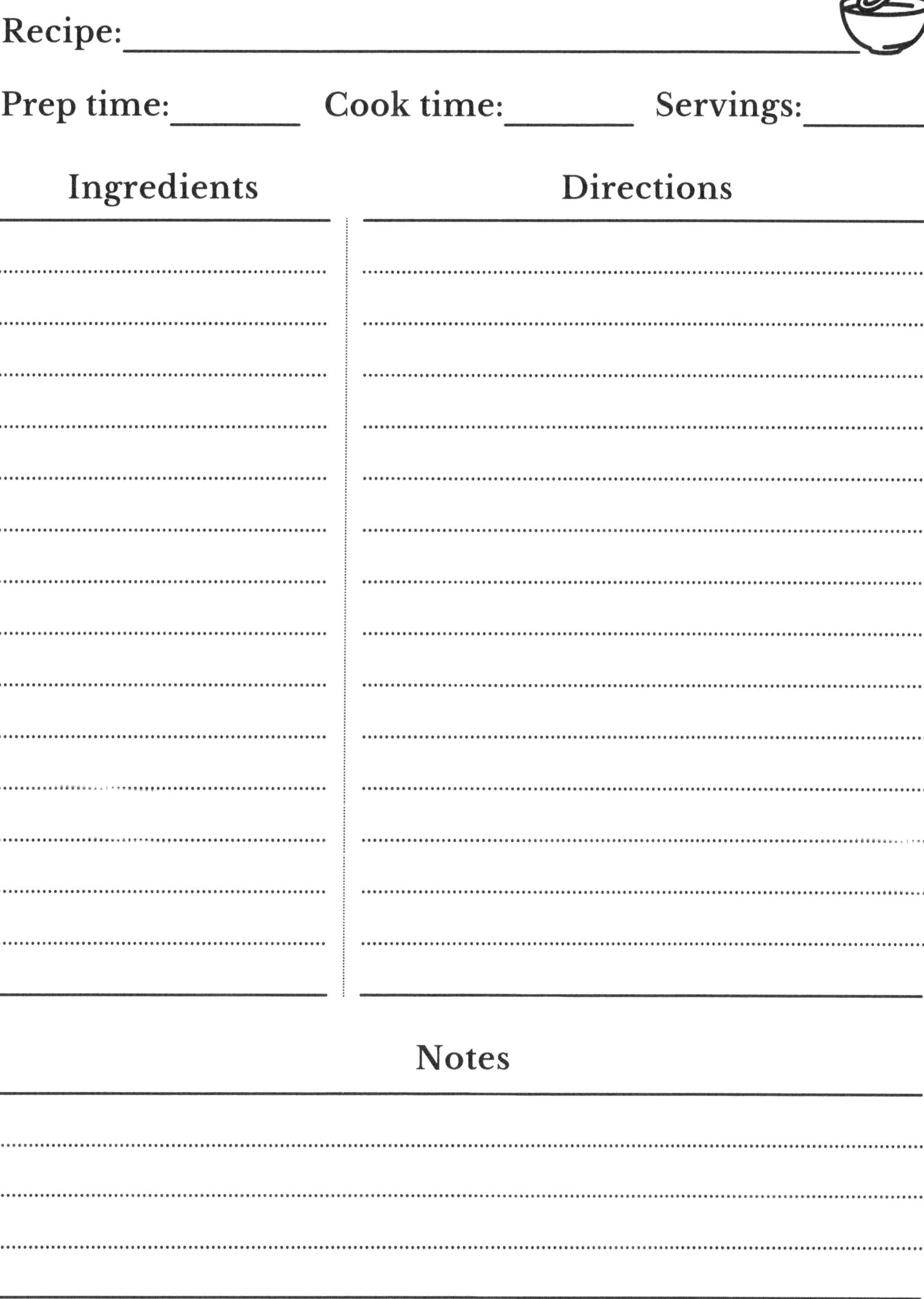

Recipe:_______________________________________

Prep time:________ Cook time:________ Servings:________

Ingredients

Directions

Notes

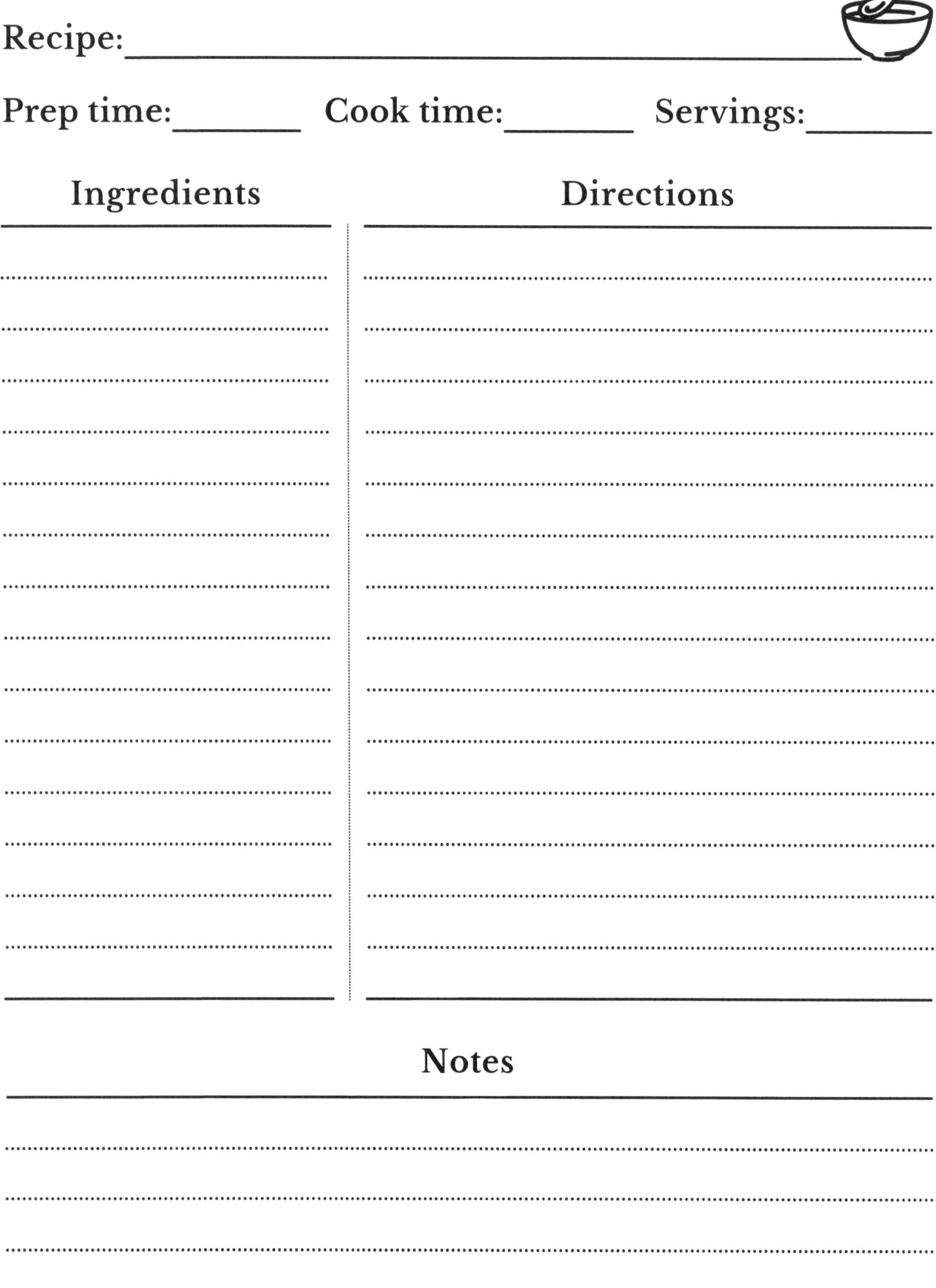

Recipe:____

Prep time:________ Cook time:________ Servings:________

Ingredients

Directions

Notes